Hazard Geography

Simon Ross

Geography teacher at
Watford Boys Grammar School

Contents

LONGMAN

CHAPTER 1

Earthquakes

What is an earthquake?

An earthquake is a violent shaking of the earth's crust. You can get an idea of what is involved from the following eye-witness account:

'We saw the earth all around heaving in a most frightful manner. The earth resembled waves coming from opposite directions and meeting in a great heap and then falling back; each time the waves seemed to fall back the ground opened slightly, and each time they met, water and sand were thrown up to a height of 18 inches or so.'
    Geological museum publication, HMSO, 1983.

The wavey motion is the result of energy waves passing through the earth. These waves are formed after a sudden snapping of the earth's crust.

Figure 1.1 shows the effect of a dropped pebble on a pond. This is similar to the effect of an earthquake. The pebble represents the snapping of the earth's crust with the ripples representing the energy waves sent out in all directions. The ripples disturb things floating on the pond; in a similar way earthquake waves will disturb buildings causing them to collapse. The largest ripples tend to be closest to the point where the pebble is dropped; in the same way, most earthquake damage is near the point of snapping, called the **focus**. This point may be a number of kilometres below the surface of the earth. The point on the surface above the focus is called the **epicentre**.

Figure 1.1 Pond ripples

How are earthquakes recorded and measured?

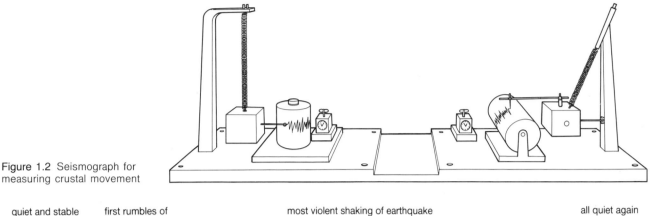

Figure 1.2 Seismograph for measuring crustal movement

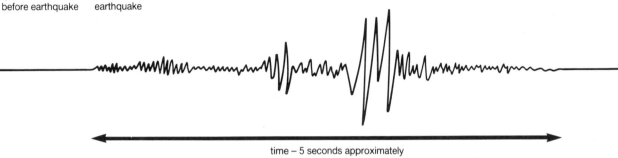

| quiet and stable before earthquake | first rumbles of earthquake | most violent shaking of earthquake | all quiet again |

time – 5 seconds approximately

Figure 1.3 A typical seismogram

Earthquakes are recorded by an instrument called a **seismograph**. This can pick up and record, by means of a line graph, the energy waves. Figure 1.2 shows a typical seismograph.

A heavy inert weight is suspended by a wire or a spring and attached to this is a pen which is in contact with paper on a revolving drum. During an earthquake the instrument frame and drum move and it is this which causes the pen to record a zig-zag line on the paper; the pen does not move.

The pattern or graph produced is called a **seismogram**. This is analysed by scientists in order to find the epicentre and strength of the earthquake. Figure 1.3 shows the seismogram recorded during a typical earthquake.

The actual power of an earthquake is measured using the **Richter scale**. Each unit on the scale represents a ×10 increase on the previous unit and although the scale does not have a limit in theory, earthquakes are rarely over 8. Figure 1.4 reveals the frequency of earthquakes of different strengths or **magnitudes**.

Magnitude on the Richter scale	Destruction	Average annual frequency
8+	great	1
7–8	major	18
6–7	destructive	120
5–6	damaging	800
4–5	minor	6,000
3–4	slightly felt	50,000
2–3	hardly noticed	300,000

Figure 1.4

ACTIVITIES

1 Sketch the seismograph shown in Figure 1.2, adding the following labels:
support frame   pen
spring/wire   rotating drum
inert weight

2 Describe in your own words how a seismograph detects and records earthquakes.

3 Can you discover the purpose of the **damping magnet**?

What is the earthquake hazard?

Figure 1.5 records some hazards resulting from earthquakes.

There are a number of immediate effects from the violent shaking of an earthquake. Buildings will collapse killing people inside them, shattered window glass will shower down on streets and huge cracks may open in the ground. Roads and railways may be damaged and services such as mains water and electricity may be cut off.

On average 15,000–20,000 people die every year as the result of earthquakes. Although this sounds a lot, it is only one-quarter of those killed in traffic accidents in the USA alone. There have been devastating earthquakes where hundreds of thousands have died. The top 5 earthquakes in terms of deaths are given below:

Date	Place	Deaths
1556	China	830,000
1737	India	300,000
1920	China	180,000
1908	Italy	160,000
1923	Japan	143,000

These figures are exceptional because, of the many thousands of earthquakes every year, only a few are centred near populated areas or are strong enough to cause loss of life. Compared to other natural disasters, the 1556 earthquake in China seems minor; the Chinese famine of 1878 claimed 9.5 million lives!

A large number of deaths occur after an earthquake, when food and medical aid are in short supply. Towns and villages in remote parts of the world (see Figure 1.5(a)) may be cut off for days because of damaged roads and railways. Services may be disrupted, preventing survivors from drinking clean water and obtaining electricity. The ability of a country to cope with an earthquake will often determine the number of deaths.

Damage to property and services can be very severe. The 1906 San Francisco earthquake caused $524 million worth of damage and the more recent 1980 southern Italy earthquake, £324 million.

Fires may start as gas or oil leaks from fractured pipes. These can sweep across towns uncontrolled as water pipes may also be broken. In 1906 fires raged for days in San Francisco following the earthquake and over 500 properties were gutted completely.

If earthquakes occur at sea or near the coast, huge waves called **tsunamis** may result. These huge waves, sometimes wrongly called tidal waves, will hit coastlines and may cause more damage than the earthquake itself. The waves can travel at speeds of 1,000 km per hour in open water, although they slow to about 65 km per hour close to land, when they reach up to 15 metres in height.

Figure 1.5a The flattened village of Calidran in Turkey following the 1976 earthquake

◀ b Collapse in Anchorage, Alaska after the 1964 earthquake

c Collapsed motorway overpass in California following the 1971 earthquake ▶

◀ d A broken main in Anchorage, Alaska

ACTIVITIES

4 Figure 1.5 shows a number of photographs of damage caused by earthquakes. Describe the general scene in each photograph and suggest the short and long-term effects in each case.

Tidal wave sweeps 100 into the Sea of Japan

From Robert Whymant in Tokyo

People in Akita stand on a collapsed wharf damaged by an earthquake and a tidal wave that hit the northern coast of Japan.

At least 100 people are dead or missing after an earthquake, followed by tidal waves up to nine feet high, hit a northern coastal area of Japan on Thursday.

Police said 30 people were known to have been killed and at least 69 were missing after being swept out to sea, including 13 primary schoolchildren on an excursion.

Two children died when they were washed away as they played on a beach during a school outing. Eleven of their playmates are missing. The rest of the party, 32 children and four adults, were rescued from the water. Sixty people were injured.

The earthquake, the strongest in 15 years, occurred shortly after noon yesterday in the Sea of Japan, off Akita Prefecture, and registered a magnitude of 7.7 on the open-ended Richter scale.

Extensive damage was reported over a wide area of Northern Japan, with roads cracked open, water main bursts, and oil leaking from ruptured pipelines.

Telephone lines in two northern prefectures were severed, railway tracks twisted in places, and the famous Bullet-train service brought to a halt.

The tidal waves – three large ones followed by smaller ones – unleashed by the earthquake caused most of the casualties. The party of primary schoolchildren was engulfed by the sea as the 41 children were picnicking on a beach in Akita Prefecture. Rescuers pulled the children from the water.

Police said many of the casualties occurred when small boats were inundated or overturned by the tidal waves. In one incident five workers at Noshiro power plant in Akita Prefecture were killed when their boat capsized. A foreign tourist, believed to be Swiss, was sucked out to sea when a wave smashed onto the seaside aquarium in the Oga peninsula, north of Akita city.

A Kyodo news service reporter, Yoshiyuki Haneda, who was at the aquarium described how the muddy brown mass of water at least six foot high swept over the aquarium parking area, carrying a number of cars out to sea. A young foreign woman was swept into the sea 'her husband tried to go after her but he was stopped by aquarium officials'.

The *Guardian*, 27 May 1983

Figure 1.6

ACTIVITIES

5 Figure 1.6 is an account of the Japanese earthquake of 26 May 1983.

   a Describe the effects of: the violent earthquake shaking and the tsunamis.

b Which do you think caused the greatest damage, the violent shaking of the earthquake or the tsunamis? Explain your answer.

Province	1 Population	2 Number of dead and injured	3 Number of dead and injured per 10,000 population	4 Number of homeless	5 Number of homeless per 1,000 population
Avellino	437,911	4,509		118,900	
Benevento	292,602	39		143,853	
Caserta	729,498	150		3,757	
Naples	2,872,348	1,564		50,446	
Salerno	1,003,427	4,115		136,853	
Matera	203,118	2		1,130	
Potenza	414,139	727		25,664	

Figure 1.7 The effects of the Southern Italian earthquake: November 1980

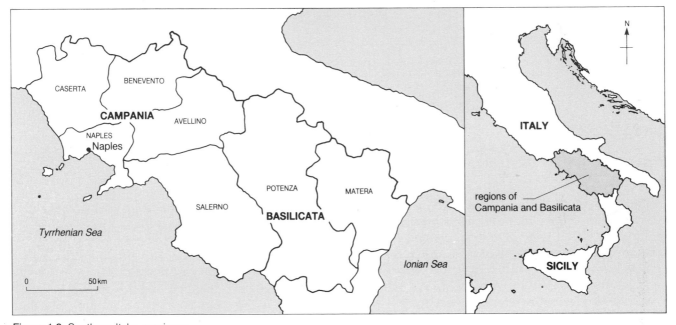

Figure 1.8 Southern Italy: provinces

ACTIVITIES

6 Figure 1.7 describes the effects of the southern Italian earthquake in November 1980.

a Complete the table shown in Figure 1.7. To find the number of dead and injured per 10,000 population, divide the number of dead and injured by the population figure and multiply your answer by 10,000.

b Why is it necessary to convert columns 2 and 4 to columns 3 and 5 respectively?

c Trace the outline map of the provinces of southern Italy (Figure 1.8). Draw a choropleth map (one using different colours or shading) for *either* column 3 or 5, making sure you give it the correct title! Use the following colour keys:

column 3	
41+	black
31–40	brown
21–30	red
11–20	orange
1–10	yellow
less than 1	white

column 5	
300+	black
251–300	dark brown
201–250	light brown
151–200	red
101–150	orange
51–100	yellow
1– 50	white

d In which province do you think the epicentre of the earthquake was?

e Why do you think Benevento suffered few deaths and injuries but had many homeless?

How are earthquakes caused?

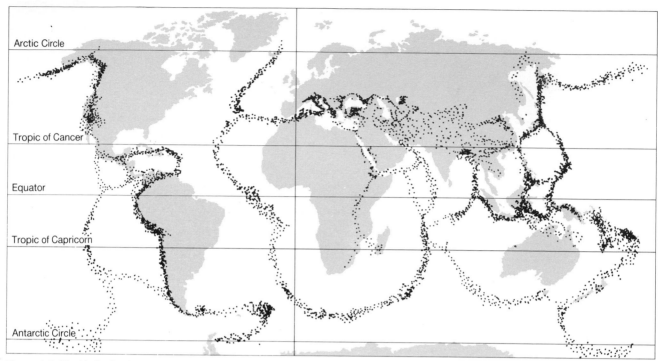

Figure 1.9 World distribution of major earthquake zones

Figure 1.9 shows the world distribution of major earthquakes. Notice that they tend to occur in a number of broad belts or zones stretching across the world. One such zone extends down the entire west coast of North and South America and another covers the centre of Europe and Asia. Earthquakes, therefore, appear to be concentrated in belts rather than occurring randomly.

During this century geologists have discovered that the earth's crust is made up of a number of **plates** up to 100 kilometres thick. These plates jostle against one another, some moving apart, some together and others sliding alongside one another. After much research the edges of these plates have been mapped and are shown in Figure 1.10. As you can see, the margins and the earthquake zones, shown in Figure 1.9, are almost identical. It is the movement of the plates which cause earthquakes at their margins.

ACTIVITIES

7 Study Figure 1.9 and, with the aid of an atlas, identify the countries and regions of the world which are most affected by earthquakes.

8 Study Figure 1.10.
  a Identify: a margin where two plates are moving apart, a margin where two plates are moving together.
  b Which of the two kinds of margins mentioned above has the most earthquakes?

9 Figure 1.11 is a list of the major earthquakes which occurred during 1983.

a Using an atlas, plot the locations on a world map. Where the location is a country, rather than a specific place, place your point approximately in the centre of the country.
b Using Figure 1.10 add the plate margins and the names of the plates to your world map.
c Which plate margins were most active during 1983?
d Which plate margins were fairly inactive during 1983?
e Were there any earthquakes a long way from a plate margin? Why do you think they occurred?

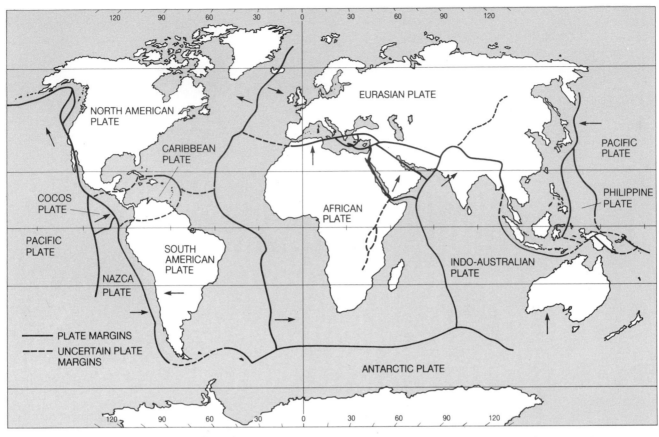

Figure 1.10 The plates of the earth's crust

8 January	Tonga Islands	10 May	New Britain, Papua New Guinea
17 January	Greece	21 June	Hokkaido, Japan
18 January	Sandwich Island	24 June	Taiwan
24 January	Mexico	5 July	Turkey
13 February	north-west China	7 July	Fiji
13 February	Mariana Island	11 July	south Shetland Island
14 February	Alaska	20 July	Sicily
25 February	Yugoslavia	2 August	France
26 February	Afghanistan/ USSR border	6 August	Pakistan
27 February	Honshu, Japan	17 August	Kamchatka, USSR
8 March	Windward Islands	4 October	north Chile
12 March	Indonesia	7 October	New York
15 March	Philippines	28 October	Idaho, USA
18 March	Papua New Guinea, New Ireland region	6 November	east China
25 March	Iran	8 November	Liège, Belgium
31 March	Colombia	9 November	north Italy
3 April	Costa Rica	16 November	Hawaii
4 April	Sumatra	30 November	Seychelles
12 April	Peru/Ecuador	2 December	Guatemala
22 April	Thailand	21 December	Argentina
2 May	central California	22 December	Guinea, north-west Africa

Figure 1.11 Some major earthquakes: 1983

Figure 1.12 The San Andreas fault

The rocks at the plate margins are put under a great deal of pressure as the plates jostle against one another. There is friction between plates at the margins which sends waves of energy outwards: an earthquake. The line along which movement occurs is called a **fault**. One of the best known faults is the San Andreas fault, which forms the margin of the Pacific and North American plates. A sudden slip along this fault caused the devastating 1906 San Francisco earthquake. There could be another slip at any time. Figure 1.12 shows part of this fault. Here a slight movement has disrupted the regular pattern of trees in a citrus grove.

As you have noted, there are earthquakes which occur away from any plate margins. These have several possible causes. Movement along old faults may give rise to earthquakes. In north-west Europe many small tremors result from underground mine collapse. During the 1970s there were many small earthquakes in Stoke-on-Trent. These created some alarm until researchers discovered that they occurred only on weekdays! They were the result of underground mining. The building of reservoirs can cause slippage along lines of weakness. For instance, there were hundreds of small tremors following the construction of the Hoover Dam in the USA. The underground disposal of liquids can lead to faults being lubricated, encouraging slippage to occur.

ACTIVITIES

10 Study Figure 1.12
   a In which direction is the fault running?
   b Which plate is to the top of the photograph, and which plate to the bottom?
   c Describe the relative movement of the two plates.
   d Does the relative movement agree with Figure 1.10?

How can we cope with earthquakes?

Although scientists have been able to identify danger areas, that is, the earthquake zones, it is not possible to evacuate them permanently. Instead there are three main ways of coping with the earthquake hazard.

Earthquake prediction

A number of scientists believe that we will soon be able to predict earthquakes, much like we forecast the weather. By studying past records of earthquakes it is possible to identify events which commonly occur just before earthquakes. These could be used as warnings of imminent earthquakes. The events include strange animal behaviour, bulging of the ground and a large number of small earth tremors.

In February 1975 such signs were present in the Haicheng area of China (see Figure 1.13) so the Government decided to evacuate over 1 million people. During the evening after the evacuation a massive earthquake, measuring 7.8 on the Richter scale, hit the area. The earthquake had been predicted successfully.

Unfortunately the Chinese could not celebrate for long. The following year 240,000 people were killed in Tangshan (see Figure 1.13) in a completely unexpected earthquake.

Thus scientists are still largely unable to predict exactly where and when earthquakes will happen.

Controlled release of pressure

As earthquakes result from the build-up of

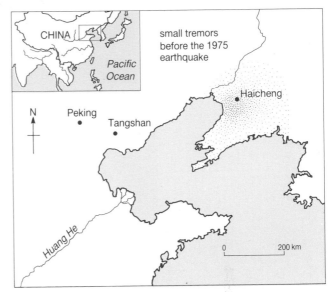

Figure 1.13 The location of Haicheng and Tangshan, China

pressure, scientists have sought ways of preventing such build-ups. Liquid has been injected into faults in Japan and the USA to lubricate and encourage gradual slipping rather than a series of sudden jerks. Some scientists believe that exploding nuclear bombs underground would work, but this would be expensive and very dangerous.

Learning to live with earthquakes

It is generally accepted that the best way of coping with earthquakes is learning to live with them. Low-lying coastal areas should be protected from tsunamis.

Figure 1.14 Rescue workers swarm over a toppled building in Mexico city following the September 1985 earthquake

Figure 1.15 Well designed peasant houses in Pakistan

More importantly, ordinary houses should be built to withstand violent shakings.

In many hot countries, such as Turkey and Iran, houses are traditionally made from sunbaked mud bricks. They have heavy roofs for insulation and no frames or supports. During earthquakes the roofs collapse and the houses may become their owners' tombs. Figure 1.5(a) shows a village of this type of housing totally destroyed.

Modern buildings can suffer just as much if they are poorly built. Figure 1.14 shows blocks of flats which were built on poor foundations; they have simply toppled over. Badly designed multi-storey buildings can collapse like a pack of cards.

In order to withstand earthquakes, buildings must have firm foundations. They must also have frames and supports made of wood or steel to give added strength and to absorb the shock waves. Figure 1.15 shows a well-built peasant house in Pakistan. Notice that it has beams of timber. Between the timbers there are thin but neat rows of carefully selected and laid rocks. The roof is fairly thin. It has also been built almost out of the hillside, giving it firm foundations.

While scientists should continue to try to predict earthquakes, inhabitants of danger areas must prepare for such events. Houses must be built properly and Governments should have temporary housing, medicine and food ready for emergencies.

ACTIVITIES

11 Read through the extract from the *Guardian* for 25 June 1981:

'This is the week of reckoning for Dr Brian Brady of the US Bureau of Mines. For almost five years now, Brady has been predicting with increasing confidence that three major earthquakes will occur this summer just off the coast of Peru, near Lima. The first one is due this weekend; and depending on whether or not it actually happens, either the United States scientific establishment or Brady himself is going to look rather silly.'

The *Guardian*, 25 June 1981.

The earthquake did not occur, much to the relief of the Peruvian Government who had decided not to evacuate the area.

a Had the Peruvian people been evacuated in June 1981, how do you think they would have reacted to future alarms?

b Discuss the advantages and disadvantages of earthquake prediction.

12 As a well respected and highly qualified housing consultant, you have been asked by a Middle Eastern Government to design earthquake-proof housing for ordinary people.

Using Figure 1.15 carefully sketch such a house. Use labels to highlight the main design features. Then, in one paragraph, describe why this type of house is safer than the traditional sunbaked mud and clay house.

CHAPTER 2

Volcanoes

What is a volcano?

A volcano is a hole (**vent**) or crack (**fissure**) in the earth's crust through which molten rock (**magma**) and hot gases escape to the surface during an **eruption**. Volcanoes often form impressive mountains.

Figures 2.1 and 2.2 show two volcanoes. Notice how the shapes of the volcanoes differ. Mount Mayon (Figure 2.1) is tall and conical whereas Mauna Loa (Figure 2.2) is broader and flatter. To understand why this is so we need to consider eruptions more carefully.

If the magma is very runny then it will come to the surface relatively gently. Once on the surface it is known as **lava**. This lava may flow

Figure 2.1 Mount Mayon, Philippines

Figure 2.2 Mauna Loa, Hawaii

for many kilometres before cooling and becoming rock. The result of this gentle eruption is a broad, flat volcano like that of Mauna Loa. Its shape gives it the name **shield** volcano.

If the magma is thick and treacle-like it requires a greater force to eject it, as old magma often blocks the vent. The eruptions tend to be violent and the lava, being thick, cools rapidly giving the volcano a tall conical shape like that of Mount Mayon. With each eruption the volcano gets bigger and bigger until a huge eruption may eventually cause the volcano to blow itself up!

Apart from lava a volcanic eruption may produce ash and larger fragments of rock (**pyroclastics**). As the pyroclastics settle on the lava the volcano takes on a layered structure. This gives the volcano the name **composite**.

To summarise, there are two main volcano shapes; broad and flat (shield), and tall and conical (composite). The difference in shape is due to the nature of the magma and the violence of the eruption.

There is a more violent eruption still that produces no lava but instead, a huge white-hot cloud of ash and gas is blasted into the air. Such a cloud is called a **nuée ardente**.

ACTIVITIES

1 Figure 2.3 is a contour map of Mount Shasta in the Cascade Mountains of the USA.

   a Draw a cross-section from X–Y. Use a vertical scale of 1 cm:1,000 metres

   b Label the following features: main volcano cone, crater of Mount Shasta, Mount Shastina – this is a *parasitic cone*.

   c Do you think that Mount Shasta is a shield or a composite volcano? Explain your answer.

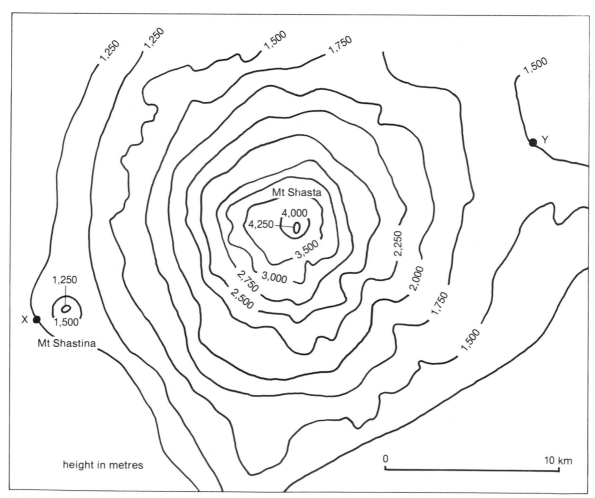

Figure 2.3 Mount Shasta, USA

What is the volcanic hazard?

There are a wide range of hazards resulting from volcanic eruptions. The ash and rocks blasted into the atmosphere can affect the weather and, on returning to the earth's surface, will cover vast areas of land with a dusty, grey blanket. A nuée ardente, will blast down the side of a volcano destroying everything in its path. If the volcano produces lava, then this will flow downhill as a river of molten rocks and gases. Tsunamis (huge 'tidal waves') may result from a particularly violent eruption.

Volcanoes would not form a hazard if people did not live so close to them, but as volcanic soils are often very fertile many people throughout the world are prepared to take a risk.

The following eruptions reveal the range of volcanic hazards.

Mount Pelée, 1902

Mount Pelée is on the Caribbean island of Martinique (see Figure 2.4). The island was a popular tourist resort at the turn of the century, with the port of St Pierre as the capital. During April 1902 the volcano started hissing and rumbling, blasting the occasional cloud of ash into the air. At the beginning of May there was another warning of possible volcanic activity, described in the following eye-witness account:

'The smell of sulphur is so strong that horses in the street stop and snort and some of them drop in their harness and die of suffocation. Many of the people are obliged to wear handkerchiefs to protect themselves from the strong smell of sulphur.'

On 8 May 1902 at 07.49 hours the volcano burst apart in a series of deafening explosions. By 07.52 hours the whole of St Pierre lay smouldering and only two of the 28,000 inhabitants remained alive! A nuée ardente had swept downhill like a ball of fire at 180 miles per hour. A man on a ship in the harbour wrote:

'The mountain was blown to pieces. The side of the volcano was ripped out and then hurled straight towards us a solid wall of flame. The wave of fire was on us and over us like a lightning flash. It was like a hurricane of fire which rolled in mass straight down on St Pierre and the shipping.'

The town was reduced to rubble and charcoal. The temperature had probably exceeded 700°C for glass was melted and iron bars were twisted.

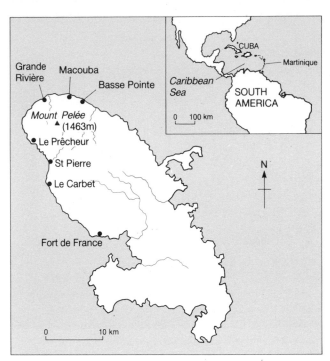

Figure 2.4 Martinique in the Caribbean

	Effects
St Pierre	28,000 people killed: nuées; tsunamis; ash falls
Macouba	ash falls; fires
Grande Rivière	many killed; mud flows
Le Carbet	fires; tsunamis
Le Prêcheur	many killed; ash falls; mud flows
Basse Pointe	tsunamis; ash falls; mud flows

Figure 2.5 The effects of the Mount Pelée eruption 1902

ACTIVITIES

2 Figure 2.5 lists some of the effects of the 1902 eruption:
   a Make a copy of the map in Figure 2.4.
   b Title your map: The effects of the 1902 Mount Pelée eruption.
   c Devise a symbol for each effect – deaths, tsunamis, mudflows, etc. – show these in a key. By referring to the table (Figure 2.5) use the correct symbol(s) to show the effects of the eruption on each town.
   d Draw a large arrow from Mount Pelée to St Pierre to show the direction of the main blast.

3 a How far is St Pierre from Mount Pelée?
   b Assuming that the main nuée ardente travelled at 300 kilometres per hour, how long did it take to reach St Pierre?

Figure 2.6 St Pierre after the 1902 eruption

Mount Vesuvius, AD 79

In the first century the Roman Empire was strong
and there were many thriving towns, such as
Pompeii, along the shores of what is now the
Bay of Naples (see Figure 2.7). In the years
leading up to AD 79 there were a number of
tremors and rumbles in the Mount Vesuvius area
but, as the local population were convinced the
volcano was extinct, no-one was unduly worried.

On 24 August Vesuvius exploded into life,
sending a huge cloud of ash into the air. This
cloud plunged Pompeii into total darkness and
ash rained down on the town. Pliny the Younger
described the scene in a series of letters. The
following is an account based on these letters:

'The darkness was so complete that Pliny compared
it with a sealed room in which the lamp had been put
out. It was much more unnerving than that though,
for they were not in a sealed room but out in the open
with the air full of cries from the crowd: screams of
terror and prayers for deliverance. The ash fall became
heavier, piling up around them, so that every now and
again they had to shake themselves clear of it, to
prevent themselves from being buried.'

Probably about 2,000 people died in Pompeii,
mostly from suffocation due to the sulphur fumes
and ash filling the air. The town was blanketed
with 3 metres of ash by the time the air cleared.

Recently Pompeii has been excavated, revealing

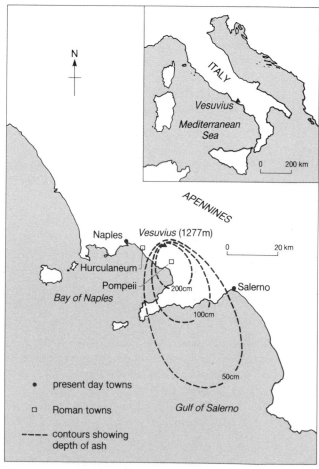

Figure 2.7 The eruption of Vesuvius AD 79

Figure 2.8 The cast of a human victim killed by the Vesuvius eruption in AD79

some of the buildings and even imprints of human corpses. These imprints have been filled carefully with plaster of Paris, producing exact replicas of the people that formed them. Figure 2.8 shows such a replica.

Krakatoa, 1883

On 27 August 1883 the island of Krakatoa in Indonesia (see Figure 2.9) literally blew itself up. The explosions could be heard almost 5,000 kilometres away as huge clouds of dust and rocks were blasted into the atmosphere. The most devastating effect of the eruption was the large number of tsunami. These huge waves, up to 35 metres high, swept along the coast of Java and Sumatra, drowning over 36,000 people.

El Chichon, 1982

In April 1982 El Chichon in Mexico erupted, sending millions of tonnes of ash into the atmosphere, where it circled the globe affecting weather in many parts of the world. The wet month of June 1982 in Britain is thought to have been a result of this eruption.

Apart from increasing rainfall, dust in the atmosphere can block out the sun, so making the earth cooler than normal. Some scientists believe that volcanic activity may have led to the last Ice Age, although this is difficult to prove.

Figure 2.9 The eruption of Krakatoa in 1883

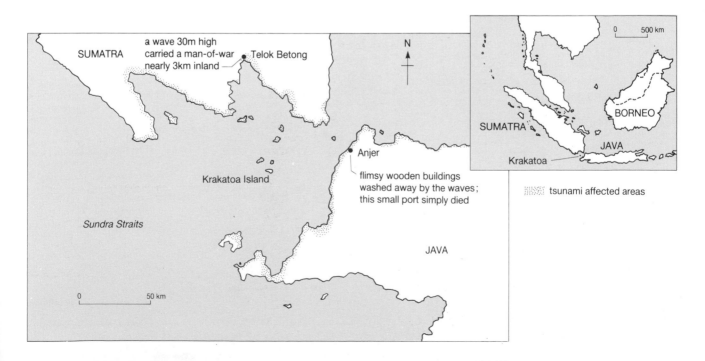

ACTIVITIES

6 Figure 2.10 is a series of maps plotting the gradual spread of the dust cloud resulting from the eruption of El Chichon.

  a How long did it take for the cloud to circle the world?

  b Between which lines of latitude did the cloud extend?

c Which countries were most affected by the cloud during April 1982?

d As you have read, scientists thought that the ash cloud affected weather in Britain in June 1982. What must have happened to the cloud since April for this to be so?

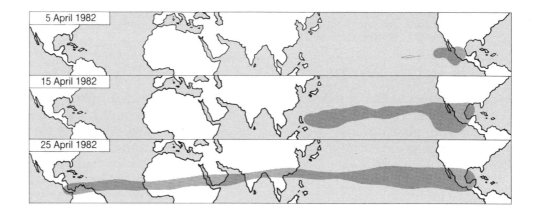

Figure 2.10 The spread of ash from El Chichon 1982

How are volcanoes formed?

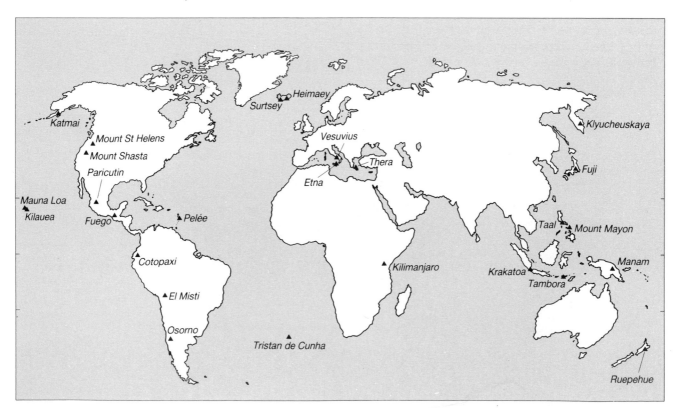

Figure 2.11 Major volcanoes of the world

7 Using Figures 2.11 and 1.10 match the volcanoes with their plate margins:

1 Heimaey	A Pacific/Eurasian
2 Klyucheuskaya	B Caribbean/South American
3 El Misti	C North American/Pacific
4 Mount Pelée	D North American/Eurasian
5 Mount Shasti	E South American/Nazca
6 Krakatoa	F Philippine/Eurasian
7 Mount Mayon	G Eurasian/Indo-Australian

8 Which volcano occurs on an **uncertain plate margin**?

9 Explain in your own words how a volcano may form other than at a plate margin.

Figure 2.11 shows the location of some of the world's major volcanoes. Look back to your map of major earthquakes. Notice that they seem to occur in much the same areas. This is because volcanoes tend to occur at the edges of the **plates** which make up the earth's surface.

Figure 2.12 explains in more detail the different ways that volcanoes can form. Notice that there are two types of plate margin, **destructive**, where old plate is being destroyed, and **constructive**, where new plate is being formed.

At the destructive margins composite volcanoes form, e.g. Mount Pelée and Krakatoa. These may form islands, as the Philippines, or may occur within mountain ranges, such as Cotopaxi in the Andes.

At constructive margins magma seeps into cracks, forming the gentler shield volcanoes. In areas where the plate is particularly thin a **hot spot** is formed and magma may escape to the surface, also forming shield volcanoes. The best example of a hot spot is Hawaii.

Figure 2.12 The formation of volcanoes

	1	2	3	4
Margin type:	destructive	'hot spot'	constructive	destructive
Volcano type:	composite	shield	usually shield	composite
Eruption:	explosive	gentle oozing	usually gentle	explosive
Products:	nuées, ash, lava	lava	lava, ash	nuées, ash, lava
Example: margin/plate : volcano	Pacific/Eurasian Fuji, Japan	Pacific Mauna Loa, Hawaii	N. American/Eurasian Surtsey, Iceland	Nazca/S. American Cotopaxi

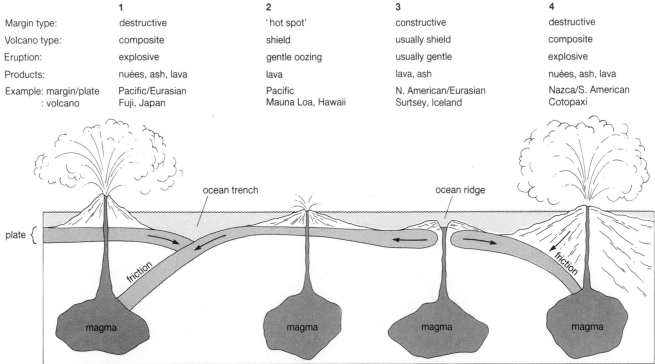

Formation: At a destructive margin one plate dives beneath the other. Friction causes it to melt and become molten magma. The magma forces its way up to the surface to form a volcano to the side of the actual plate margin (the ocean trench). A number of volcanoes may reach the surface to form a string of islands called an **island arc** e.g. the Philippines.

In places where a plate is particularly thin magma may be able to escape to the surface. Such a place is called a '**hot spot**'. A shield volcano will be formed like those on Hawaii.

Where two plates are moving apart new magma can reach the surface through the gap. Volcanoes forming along this crack create a submarine mountain range called an ocean ridge e.g. Mid-Atlantic ridge.

Sometimes destructive margins involve continents. Instead of forming islands volcanoes occur within a range of mountains e.g. Andes.

Can the volcanic hazard be reduced?

A volcanic eruption can not be stopped. However, the dangers of an eruption can be reduced, either by prediction or by swift action after an eruption has started.

Prediction

A study of historical records suggests that volcanoes 'warm up' before erupting. Scientists have discovered a number of 'symptoms' that occur just prior to eruptions.

In the months leading up to the 1980 eruption of Mount St Helens in the USA, there were a number of events:

March 1980   many small earthquakes in the Mount St Helens area.

April 1980   many small eruptions formed fresh craters.

May 1980   a large bulge, some 100 metres high, appeared on the north face; snow and ice on the mountain melted; local farm animals behaved strangely.

18 May 1980   major eruption following a strong earthquake.

However, while scientists were sure that an eruption would occur, they were unable to predict exactly when it would be or how serious it would be. Even after evacuation and the 'sealing off' of large areas of land some people lost their lives.

ACTIVITIES

10 With reference to the Mount St Helens eruption, try to explain:
    a the cause of the 100 metre bulge,
    b the melting of snow and ice on the mountain,
    c the lost of life even after the precautions taken.

11 Figure 2.13 shows Mt St Helens just beginning to erupt. Make a sketch of Figure 2.13 and label some of the features of the eruption.

12 In 1976 70,000 people were evacuated from the area around the La Soufriere volcano on the Caribbean island of Guadeloupe as it showed signs of a likely eruption. However, it proved to be a false alarm. How might this false alarm cause problems for scientists in the future?

Figure 2.13 Mount St Helens just beginning to erupt in 1980

Action following an eruption

Apart from the risk of asphyxiation, a serious ash hazard is the additional weight put on buildings, often leading to their collapse. To prevent this, roofs can be strengthened or people evacuated, if necessary.

Against lava rather more can be done. In 1935 bombs were used to divert the flow of lava from the town of Hilo on Hawaii. More recently, during the 1973 eruption of Helgafell on Iceland, sea water was hosed onto the lava when it threatened the town of Vestmannaeyjar. This cooled the lava from 1,000°C to 100°C, causing it to solidify before reaching the town. Figure 2.14 shows lava spraying.

Figure 2.14 Spraying advancing lava in Iceland

ACTIVITIES

13 Read the newspaper article in Figure 2.15 which describes the most recent attempt to divert lava. Under the title 'Diverting lava on Mount Etna':

  a Describe the eruption and its effects on the local area. Why did the lava need to be diverted?

  b Using diagrams describe how the explosive engineers intended to divert the lava flow.

14 After a number of technical problems the diversion attempt took place on 14 May 1983. Figure 2.16 records its results.

  a Lennart describes the operation as a 'complete success'. Do you agree?

  b How might politics have influenced the decision to divert the lava?

  c List some of the difficulties when attempting to divert lava flow.

Figure 2.15 Diverting lava on Mount Etna 1983

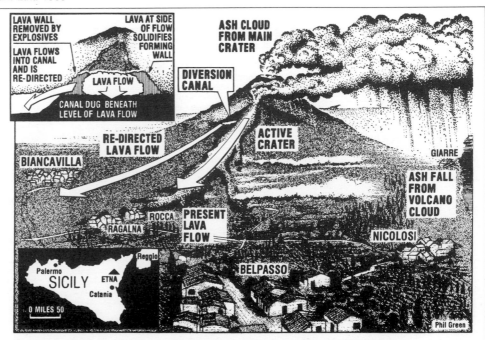

Etna's path of destruction and the course the engineers plan for the lava

Figure 2.15 continued

Dynamite gang to tame volcano

continued from previous page

MOUNT ETNA, Europe's largest volcano, now in full eruption, is to undergo major surgery on Wednesday. In what has been described as "the first example of volcanic engineering in history", it is hoped to deviate and slow down a torrent of lava threatening villages on the volcano's lower slopes.

The eruption began 42 days ago in the side of the mountain at 7,770 feet. Since then, millions of tons of lava have gushed out of a small crater and covered the mountainside with immense tongues of molten rock – some of them up to 3¾ miles long – which can be seen at night from Catania. So far, one hotel, three restaurants, 25 houses and numerous orange groves have been swallowed up. Last Monday, the main crater of Etna's 11,231 ft summit began to erupt.

There is only one other recorded example of an attempt at volcanic engineering. In 1944, the United States Air Force was called in to bomb the crater of an erupting volcano in Hawaii. It was hoped to open a breach in the crater so that lava, threatening an inhabited area, would flow out in the opposite direction. The experiment failed totally.

For centuries, Etna's mountain-dwellers tried to divert lava flows from their houses and farms, then in the 19th century this was made illegal. Last week, Orazio Nicoloso, the doyen of Etna's mountaineers, told The Sunday Times that during an eruption in 1971, he flouted the law. One night with friends, using bull-dozers, he successfully diverted a lava flow that was threatening a cable-car station. Nicoloso's achievement became widely known and was probably a factor in convincing the Italian authorities 10 days ago to change the law and take action.

The lava pouring out from the side of the mountain has carved out a channel for itself about 20ft wide and 15ft deep with ridges of solidified lava forming on either side of its course. The lava races along at an average of about 10mph. After about half a mile it begins to slow down.

As in an operation to divert a river, the intention is to blow up a section of the solidified ridge and channel the molten lava along a new path. There is frenetic activity at the scene. The technicians spend most of their time at the part to be blown up. There, at a level about 10ft below the molten rock, a section has been dug out for the explosive charges to be placed.

Nearby more than 100 men, using lorries, 15 mechanised shovels and five bulldozers, are working in a biting wind and swirling sulphur clouds, preparing a canal for the lava. It is hoped that the lava will burst into the canal after the explosion, then run into an ancient crater and down the mountainside parallel to the present flows.

The lava wall will be blown up by a Swedish explosives engineer . . . , with an Italian colleague, Giovanni Ripamonte. They will have to place by hand at least 40 high-explosive charges in the wall at a very high temperature.

The danger will be enormous for the two men. They will have only two minutes before the explosion to dash for a shelter 280 yards away.

The Sunday Times, 8 May 1983

Figure 2.16 The diversion of lava – success or failure?

How Rolf turned the tide of history

by Dalbert Hallenstein

AT nine minutes past four yesterday morning, to the sound of a military trumpet, Mount Etna was attacked with rockets and bombs. The immense effort, to alter the course of a lava torrent, was a qualified failure.

The huge explosion, the world's first example of volcanic engineering, caused only a partial deviation of the fast flow: Scientists said it may take days to determine whether the plan to divert the lava into a man-made canal and away from inhabited areas has worked.

Some eminent Italians are not only disappointed in the result, but admit that the villages the explosion was expected to save had been in no real danger, anyway.

However, Rolf Lennart, the Swedish explosives expert in charge of the blasting, said he considered the operation "a complete success, considering the circumstances".

Lennart said the constant flux in the depth of the lava forced him and his team to change plans continually. He said the lava kept splashing over a restraining wall, damaging metal tubes that were to hold the dynamite and doubling the wall's thickness in two days to nearly 19 ft.

Renato Cristofolini, professor of vulcanology at Catania university, who helped prepare the attempted diversion, said: "We were asked by the Ministry of Civil Protection for our opinion. The original request for the project came from the Etna villagers. We agreed to help, but I admit the decision to go ahead was partly political."

What he meant was that there will be elections on June 26 and the local mayors saw a successful onslaught on the volcano as a useful campaign weapon.

The explosives technicians took terrible risks placing the charges in the lava wall. There was the constant peril of a lava slip burning them to death. But they also had to worry about a spontaneous explosion resulting from a temperature of 50 degC in the wall itself.

At 4am yesterday, the hundreds of technicians and journalists on the erupting volcano were ordered to lie down in sand-bagged bunkers, which had also been designed as grandstands. This was followed by the sound of the trumpet as a warning of the coming explosion.

At first it seemed that the explosion had completely failed. But as the dust and smoke cleared, glowing lava could be seen bursting out of the breach. The original lava flow began to slow down but then suddenly speeded up again to its former 10 miles an hour, and after more than three hours, the new flow had reached only 350 yards.

Lava has been pouring out of a crater from the summit of the 10,700 ft volcano nearly five miles down the south-eastern slope.

Cristofolini said the aim of the attempted diversion was to "buy time because the diverted lava will eventually rejoin the natural stream further downhill". The project was to slow the natural course by two weeks or so.

He said three nearby towns including Ragalna, nearly a mile away were in no danger even if the canal was not built, because the lava was slowing.

The Sunday Times, 15 May 1983

CHAPTER 3

Flooding

What is flooding?

A flood is a body of water which rises to overflow land not normally submerged.

The photograph in Figure 3.1 shows an area of land that has been flooded. Flooding is quite common; hardly a week goes by without reference by the media to a flood somewhere in the world. Such newspaper and television reports always highlight the tragedy involved.

Although damage to property and loss of life illustrate the dangers of flooding, it is important to remember that throughout history some types of flooding have been highly beneficial.

Until recently the River Nile in Egypt flooded every year, between June and September laying a thick blanket of rich, black sediment on the adjacent floodplain. This sediment was fertile; so improving farming in the area. This is one reason why the Nile area has been relatively densely populated. The construction in 1964 of the Aswan High Dam has deprived most of the floodplain of its annual free fertiliser.

ACTIVITIES

1 Figure 3.1 shows a flood in lowland Britain. Carefully study the photograph. As you can see, it is not so much a disaster as an inconvenience.
Using the bridges as guides, try to identify the normal course of the river.

a Describe the effects of the flood on: agricultural land, communications (roads, etc.), housing.

b What sort of problems do you think ordinary householders would have to cope with during flooding and immediately after flooding?

2 As a class, collect information on recent floods in order to produce a display. You can obtain information from newspapers or television reports. Plot the location of the floods on a world map. Show the damage caused (deaths, financial loss, etc.) using bargraphs.

Figure 3.1 Flooding of the River Stour near Blandford

Why is flooding a hazard?

If the land next to rivers and the sea was left completely alone, flooding would not be a hazard. But, due to the development of floodplains for housing, transport routes and agriculture, flooding may cause many problems to man.

Apart from the loss of life, property may be damaged or even completely destroyed.

Agricultural land may be flooded, ruining crops and killing livestock. Transport may be disrupted and settlements cut off by floodwater. Services such as water, electricity and gas may be affected. Other less obvious but equally important hazardous effects include loss of working hours, inconvenience and anxiety. Figure 3.2 gives some examples of the flood hazard.

Figure 3.2 Some examples of the flood hazard

a

In Florence, Italy, on 4 November 1966 a 130 kilometres per hour wave rushed through the streets destroying 10,000 cars and making 5,000 people homeless. Thirty-three inhabitants were killed; electricity, water and sewage were cut off; and many priceless art treasures, including 300,000 rare books and 1,300 paintings, were ruined. The cost of reconstruction exceeded 300 million pounds.

b

Flooding by Yangtze threatens millions

Peking (Reuter) – Millions of people struggled yesterday to stop the Yangtze river sending floodwaters cascading through one of China's most heavily populated regions.

Torrential rain has pushed a 900-mile stretch of the country's biggest river to critical levels in five provinces, and official reports spoke of desperate efforts to shore up dykes and drain flooded areas.

The *China Daily* said at least two people died in the eastern province of Anhui in floods which brought down power lines, cut off water supplies and engulfed great areas of farmland. The paper quoted the *Anhui Daily* as saying a community of 3,000 peasants had been stranded.

The rain began last week and was still falling yesterday. Officials predicted the Yangtze would rise even higher as water poured off the mountains of south-west Sichuan province.

The Times, 12 July 1983

c

The London Borough of Hammersmith and Fulham 'Flood Survival' brochure reads:
'*Floods in London would be catastrophic. Many thousands of homes would be affected, and the lives of those people who had ignored the warnings seriously endangered. Essential services would be stretched to the limit, and people would have to fend for themselves . . . residents could be without electricity, gas and telephone for some days . . . and it is possible that all areas could be affected by a back flow (of sewage) from the drains, through gullies, water closets, baths, basins or sinks.*'

d
Deaths resulting from historic flood disasters: 1642–1972

Country	Number of deaths
China	4,806,500
Japan	40,000
USA	4,125
Pakistan and India	2,700
Italy	2,113
Iran	2,000
Brazil	900
Haiti	500
Spain	470
Portugal	457
France	412
England	284
Rumania	200

ACTIVITIES

3 The most obvious way of removing the flood hazard is for man to leave the floodplains completely free of development. Discuss some of the reasons why this is impractical.

4 Using the examples referred to above, list some of the results of flooding and place them in order of importance. Give reasons for your order.

5 Figure 3.2(d) shows the death toll resulting from major floods. China is by far the most severely hit. This is due to a number of factors. China has a very large population, most of whom live in lowland river basins. Due to the climate and minimal regulation of water, flooding is common and has a serious effect on those living close to the rivers.

Undertake a short project on the flood hazard in China. Include the following:

a Draw a map to show relief, drainage and population distribution. Try to explain the population distribution. Describe why the population distribution means that flooding may lead to great loss of life.

b Describe the climate of China. Does it increase the flood risk? Why?

c If possible give some actual examples of floods in China. Show their locations on a map and list the effects of flooding. The newspaper article, Figure 3.2(b), will start you off.

How are floods caused?

Although floods can occur as the result of a variety of causes (dam bursts, coastal flooding, tidal waves, pipe bursts, etc.), the most common cause is an excessive amount of rainwater flooding inland river floodplains.

In order to understand how this occurs we can consider the water in a drainage basin as a system, the **drainage basin hydrological system**. **Precipitation** forms the **input** into the system. When it falls onto a drainage basin a number of things may happen. It may return to the atmosphere through evaporation from the ground surface and through transpiration from plants, which together form an **output** from the system called **evapotranspiration**.

When water gathers on the ground **infiltration** may occur. This is when the soil soaks up water. The speed of infiltration is called the **infiltration rate**.

Once in the soil water moves quite slowly, either near the surface as **throughflow** or much deeper as **groundwater flow**. The upper surface of the groundwater zone is termed the **water-table** (see Figure 3.3).

Figure 3.3 The drainage basin hydrological system

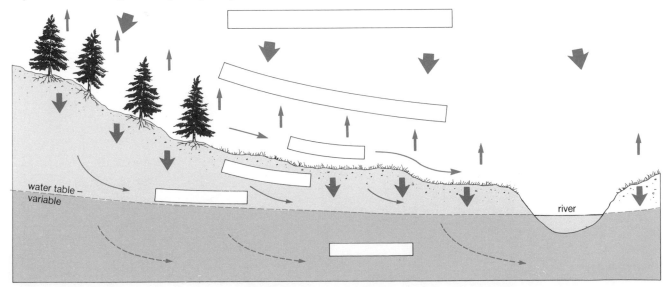

Any water that does not infiltrate moves rapidly downhill on the ground surface and is called **overland flow**. It is this that is most commonly responsible for causing floods.

After a period of infiltration, the water table will rise. This will reduce the available pore spaces in the soil and bedrock so making overland flow more likely. If the water table should reach the surface then overland flow will also occur.

The flood hydrograph

The amount of water flowing down a river is called its **discharge**. This is measured at a particular location in units of **cubic metres per second**. Discharges over a period of time can be plotted on a graph to produce a **hydrograph**. This is usually drawn to show the effect of a storm, when it becomes known as a **storm hydrograph**. Figure 3.4 shows a typical storm hydrograph. Notice that the discharge rises quite rapidly after a rain storm, although there is a time lag between peak rainfall and peak discharge. After the peak, the discharge decreases gradually. Note too that the graph can be sub-divided into **normal flow** and **storm flow**.

ACTIVITIES

6 Copy Figure 3.3 and fill in the empty boxes. You will find the missing labels amongst the terms in bold print in the text describing the drainage basin hydrological system. Also include a key to show what each type of arrow indicates.

7 Why is overland flow usually responsible for sudden floods?

8 Overland flow only happens when water can not infiltrate fast enough into the soil. In other words, the infiltration rate is exceeded by precipitation.
   For each of the following conditions say whether you would expect the infiltration rate to be rapid (flooding unlikely) or slow (flooding likely) and explain why:
   a frozen soil
   b wet clay soil
   c dry sandy soil
   d tarmac or concrete-covered surface
   e densely vegetated area
   f wet soil with high water table

ACTIVITIES

9 a On graph paper copy Figure 3.5(a). Plot the discharge values for 1–12 November (3.5(b)). Join the points with a freehand curve to produce a storm hydrograph. Use Figure 3.4 to help you sub-divide the graph into normal and storm flow.
   b What is the time lag between peak rainfall and peak discharge?
   c Authorities whose duty it is to issue flood alerts study hydrographs very carefully. Why is this?
   d Which type of water movement (overland flow, throughflow or groundwater flow) accounts for the following, do you think?: rapid rising limb and peak, gradual falling limb, normal flow. Give reasons for your answers.

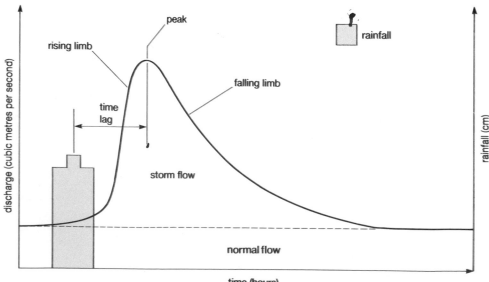

Figure 3.4 Typical flood hydrograph

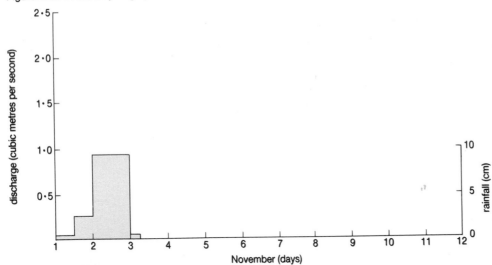

Figure 3.5a A flood hydrograph for 1–12 November

b Discharge figures taken at 12.00 (noon) 1–12 November

Date	Discharge (cubic metres per second)
1	0·050
2	0·050
3	0·400
4	2·500
5	1·600
6	0·700
7	0·400
8	0·300
9	0·250
10	0·225
11	0·200
12	0·170

Figure 3.6 describes with examples the main causes of flooding. Read through it and attempt the activities on page 30.

Figure 3.6 The causes of floods

Cause

Dam failure
The collapse of a dam tends to result from human error, for instance, the construction of the dam on weak rock.
  There are, however, times when tectonic activity may lead to dam failure.
  Dam failure, although dramatic, is rare.

Example

In 1928 the **St Francis Dam** in California, USA, collapsed killing 500 people.
  The worst flood in the USA occurred in 1889 when a dam burst led to over 2,000 people being drowned in Johnsville, Pennsylvannia.
  The worst flood in the UK also resulted from a dam burst; in 1864 200 people died in Sheffield.

Cause

Snowmelt
Snow acts as a water store. Precipitation occurs but is stored as snow on the surface. When it melts there is a sudden release of water which may lead to flooding.
  One metre of snow is equivalent to 83 mm of rainfall.
  Snow melts at varying rates:
 65 mm/day – warm air only.
175 mm/day – warm air and sunshine.
250 mm/day – warm air and rainfall.

Example

Britain 1946–47
The winter of 1946–47 was very severe. There was over 1 metre of snow covering the Pennines, with drifts up to 5 metres deep.
  On 10 March 1947 temperatures rose rapidly from 0°C to 10°C in only a few hours. Combined with steady rainfall, snow began to melt and very serious flooding resulted.
  Parts of the rivers Thames, Severn, Wye, Conwy and Dee flooded, causing the deaths of thousands of sheep and lambs.
  Areas of the West Country, Midlands, Yorkshire and East Anglia were affected. Thousands of acres of prime agricultural land in the Fens were under water.
  Many towns were inundated: Nottingham, Bath, Reading, Tewkesbury, Shrewsbury, Tonbridge, Rotherham, Doncaster, Gainsborough and Goole, for example.

Before the Lynmouth flood, 1952

After the Lynmouth flood, 1952

Cause

Rainstorm

A heavy rainstorm or long wet period causes the soil to become saturated. There is too much water to infiltrate into the soil; the infiltration rate is exceeded. The result is surface runoff which may cause a flood. Heavy storms occur in the summer, usually as the result of the intense heat.

The heaviest storm in Britain was at Martinstown, Dorset, when 297.4 mm fell in 24 hours on 18 July 1955.

Example

Lynmouth, Devon, 1952

Perhaps the most dramatic flood resulting from heavy rainfall occurred in August 1952 in the small, north Devon resort of Lynmouth.

During the first two weeks of August almost continuous rain had saturated the soil. On 15 August 228 mm fell in 24 hours. This was transferred to the rivers as runoff and led to a tremendous surge of water tumbling down the steep valley floors.

Almost the entire High Street was removed by floodwaters which carried 91 houses and 100 vehicles out to sea. In total 34 people died and 200,000 tonnes of boulders were swept into the town. The following quote tells of the tragedy:

'It was thought that one of the bridges . . . must have collapsed, for the water rose rapidly and began to fill the cottages. The sole remaining and aged occupants must have realised their terrible position and their agony of mind does not bear thinking about. The anxious and helpless watchers at the school saw a light burning in the bedroom which they occupied, up to midnight. Then that light went out . . .

A particularly violent roar at 1.20 a.m. was heard above the general tumult . . . it is believed to have been the time when the houses were swept into the fury of the flood.'

Cause

Coastal flooding

Coastal flooding is the inundation of coastal areas by sea water. It occurs when high tides and severe weather out to sea combine to raise the sea above the level of coastal defences.

It may also result from earthquakes, volcanoes and hurricanes, as covered in other chapters.

Example

Eastern England, 31 January 1953

In total over 800 square kilometres of land was flooded by salt water, causing about 50 million pounds worth of damage. Over 300 people lost their lives, 35,000 were evacuated and Canvey Island was swamped. As you can see from the text on the map opposite, when severe storms hit the east coast in 1978, although much damage was done, only one person died.

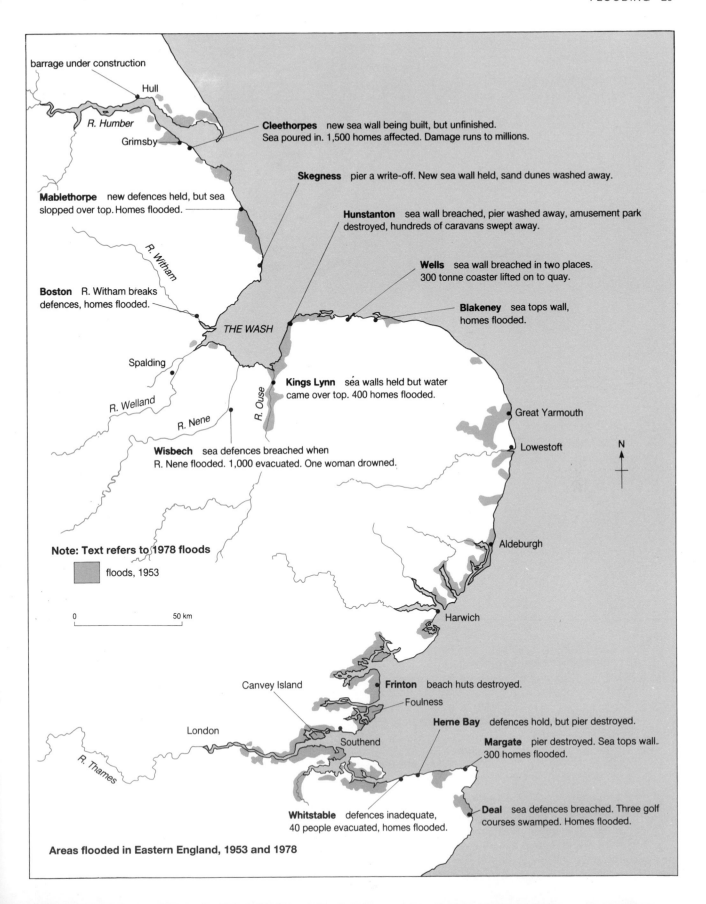

barrage under construction

Hull

R. Humber

Grimsby

Cleethorpes new sea wall being built, but unfinished. Sea poured in. 1,500 homes affected. Damage runs to millions.

Skegness pier a write-off. New sea wall held, sand dunes washed away.

Mablethorpe new defences held, but sea slopped over top. Homes flooded.

R. Witham

Hunstanton sea wall breached, pier washed away, amusement park destroyed, hundreds of caravans swept away.

Wells sea wall breached in two places. 300 tonne coaster lifted on to quay.

Boston R. Witham breaks defences, homes flooded.

Blakeney sea tops wall, homes flooded.

THE WASH

Spalding

R. Welland

R. Nene

R. Ouse

Kings Lynn sea walls held but water came over top. 400 homes flooded.

Great Yarmouth

Lowestoft

N

Wisbech sea defences breached when R. Nene flooded. 1,000 evacuated. One woman drowned.

Note: Text refers to 1978 floods

floods, 1953

Aldeburgh

0   50 km

Harwich

Canvey Island

Frinton beach huts destroyed.

Foulness

Herne Bay defences hold, but pier destroyed.

London

Margate pier destroyed. Sea tops wall. 300 homes flooded.

Southend

R. Thames

Whitstable defences inadequate, 40 people evacuated, homes flooded.

Deal sea defences breached. Three golf courses swamped. Homes flooded.

Areas flooded in Eastern England, 1953 and 1978

Figure 3.7 Town plans of Lynmouth before and after flooding, 1952

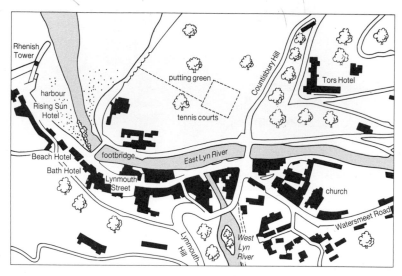

a Before flooding

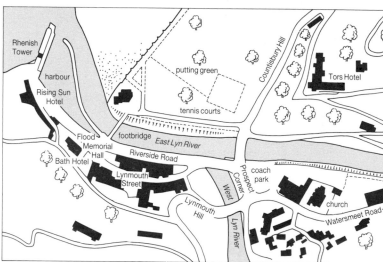

b After flooding

ACTIVITIES

10 Figure 3.7 shows the difference in the town of Lynmouth following the flood there.
   a What buildings are missing from the present town plan, presumably destroyed by the flood?
   b What changes have taken place in: road layout and bridges, river course and width, land uses immediately next to the river?
   c What evidence is there in Figure 3.7(b) to suggest that deliberate planning should prevent such a disaster ever occurring again?

11 In Figure 3.6 (page 27) different rates of snowmelt are given. Why do you think these variations occur?

12 On an outline map of Great Britain, mark the following, using an appropriate key. Title your map 'The snowmelt floods in Britain 1946–7'.

   a Pennine Hills (where 1 metre of snow lay),
   b the rivers which flooded,
   c the areas of land affected by flooding,
   d the towns inundated.

13 With reference to an Ordnance Survey map (of North Wales or northern England, for example) locate an important reservoir and dam. With the aid of a sketch map write an imaginary account of the effects of a dam collapse on the surrounding area.

14 Study the map on page 29 and make a list of the different kinds of damage caused by the 1978 floods. For one of the locations mentioned, write a front page newspaper article, using eye witness accounts and sketches.

Can the flood hazard be reduced?

It is possible to predict a likely flood by using satellites and radar to show up rainfall and soil moisture. Storm hydrographs are widely used in the study of flooding. However, such warnings will give only a few hours notice to the public to prepare for a flood.

Engineers planning to build in flood prone areas or to strengthen flood defences study records of past floods. These enable them to work out the likelihood of floods of different sizes or **magnitudes** happening. The larger the flood, the less frequently it occurs – severe floods may occur, on average, once every 50 years. Such a flood is termed a **fifty year flood**.

Obviously towns need protection from frequent floods, but the difficulty lies in deciding whether towns should be protected from the less frequent **one hundred year floods** or even **one thousand year floods**. The greater the protection, the more expensive the operation. Most towns in Britain are protected against one hundred year floods; householders just have to hope that the one thousand year flood does not happen while they live there!

It is impossible to prevent flooding on a large scale, although protection against flooding is possible. Protection is either by non-structural **behavioural** methods or by structural **physical** methods. Figure 3.8 describes some of the more common means.

Figure 3.8 Methods of flood protection

BEHAVIOURAL

Accepting the loss This is especially common in the Third World.

Public relief funds After a disaster a fund is often set up. Following the Lynmouth flood, for example, money was sent from all over the world. At the end of the first week £151,000 had been donated and when the fund closed in the summer of 1953 over £1,300,000 had been collected.

Flood insurance It is now possible in certain areas to insure property against flood damage.

Flood forecasting and warning
In areas with a history of flooding river gauges are used to forecast floods and warnings are given to the public via the media, sirens or police loudhailers.

STRUCTURAL

Reservoirs These can be built in the upper courses of rivers to store water, so preventing sudden floods. Clywedog, Wales, has reduced flooding along much of the River Severn.

Channel enlargement Rivers can be deepened and widened, so that they are able to hold more water before they overflow.

Embankments Many towns are protected by concrete or brick embankments, which may be 2 or 3 metres high on either side of the river. They are common as they are relatively cheap to build.

Flood relief channels Artificial channels can be built around a town to take away excess water and prevent flooding.

Barrages Dams or barrages can be built across rivers, for example, the Thames barrier, but they are expensive.

Floodplain zoning Planning authorities can prohibit certain land uses in flood prone areas.

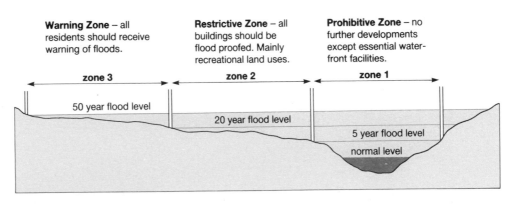

Warning Zone – all residents should receive warning of floods.

Restrictive Zone – all buildings should be flood proofed. Mainly recreational land uses.

Prohibitive Zone – no further developments except essential water-front facilities.

zone 3   zone 2   zone 1

50 year flood level

20 year flood level

5 year flood level

normal level

Floodplain zoning

ACTIVITIES

15 Why is 'accepting the loss' so common in the Third World?

16 Study the diagram showing floodplain zoning in Figure 3.8. What is meant by:

a essential waterfront activities,

b recreational land uses?

17 Figure 3.9 is map showing flooding in the fictional town of Capelby. The flood occurred after heavy rain and smowmelt during early March. The greatest flooding was in the early hours of 12th March, taking many people by surprise. Although nobody died, a number of people received minor injuries and a tremendous amount of damage was done.

a *Either* write a newspaper front page describing the flood and its effects. Use eye-witness accounts, sketches and maps. *Or* write a serious account of the Capelby flood. Refer to its causes and effects. Make up a map to show the location of the town. You should include surrounding upland areas where snow has lain. Figure 3.13 might give you some ideas.

b You have been given the job of trying to protect Capelby from future flooding. Look back at Figure 3.8 which describes the possible methods you could use.
Decide which method(s) would be most suited to Capelby.
Use a detailed map to help you describe what you intend to do.
State why you think your scheme is the best for Capelby.

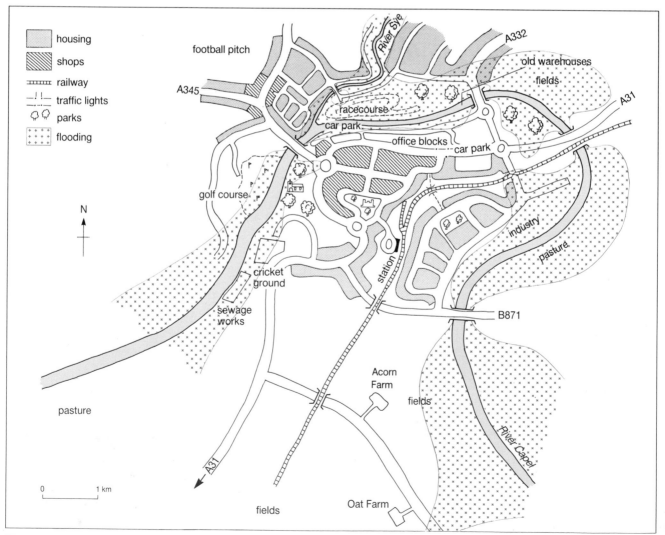

Figure 3.9 Flooding at Capelby

The Thames barrier

Why does London need protecting?

You have already read about the 1953 floods which very nearly caused disaster in London. There have been several occasions in the past when London has been flooded. Samuel Pepys wrote in December 1663 of:

'The greatest tide that ever was remembered in England to have been in this river, all Whitehall having been drowned.'

Figure 3.10 is taken from a press release by the Greater London Council.

'There is little doubt that the severe flooding of London could be the greatest natural disaster this country is likely to experience.

More than a million people who live in London's low-lying areas could be at risk and there could be loss of life. More than a quarter of a million homes, factories and offices could also be in danger. Thousands of cars would be swamped. Gas and electricity supplies could be in danger and water could become contaminated.

Transport could come to a standstill in central London. The Underground system could be paralysed for six months. Buses could operate only outside the flooded areas. Thames bridges and tunnels would be unusable.

Many areas of London might be under water for days. The Houses of Parliament could be under 3 feet of water.

The direct cost of a major flood in London could be around £3,000 million, the indirect cost being many times greater.'

Figure 3.10 Greater London Council press release

The barrier

The Thames barrier (see Fig. 3.11) spans the 520 metres of the River Thames at Silvertown in the Woolwich Reach. It consists of ten movable gates that usually rest on the river bed. These gates are raised to form a solid barrage should a high tide be forecast. Ships normally pass through the four main gates, each of which has a width of 61 metres. The gates are steel structures 20 metres high.

The cost of the scheme totalled about £484 million and the barrier was first raised in 1982. Figure 3.12 describes the workings of the barrier.

Figure 3.11 The Thames barrier

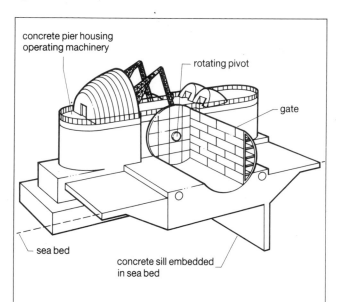

concrete pier housing operating machinery

rotating pivot

gate

sea bed

concrete sill embedded in sea bed

'If a dangerously high tide threatens an order to close is given. The engineer in charge will start operations which will result in the gates being swung through about 90° from their river bed position, forming a continuous steel wall facing downriver ready to stem the tide. Barrier closure itself would only take about 30 minutes.'

Figure 3.12 How the barrier works

ACTIVITIES

19 Write an account of the Thames barrier scheme. Describe the need for the barrier and explain, using a sketch, how it works. Refer to an atlas and draw a map showing the location of the barrier.

CASE STUDY

The York floods, 1982

York floods: an introduction

During the first few days of January 1982 Yorkshire suffered the most severe floods since March 1947 with over 800 properties and 187,000 hectares of agricultural land inundated.

In York, Selby and Boroughbridge it was necessary for the district councils to call for military assistance to carry personnel and food, evacuate residents and sandbag premises.

Causes

During December 1981 severe snowstorms affected the region, covering the Pennines with a thick blanket of snow. When temperatures rose in late December the snow began to melt. The rate of melting increased in early January as heavy rain affected Yorkshire.

The water ran quickly off the Pennines and into the rivers causing the river levels to rise rapidly.

Effects

The rapid rise in river levels caused banks to burst and overflowing. Figure 3.13 shows flooding at Cawood just south of York. Perhaps the worst hit area was between York and Selby. Figure 3.14 is a map extract of the area, to which you should refer when reading the following account from a report by the Yorkshire Water Authority:

Figure 3.13 Flooding at Cawood

'At Cawood the river overflowed the defences under construction and inundated 90 properties in the village, although the completed defences protected 20 houses in Anson Grove. Floodwater overflowed in Kelfield Ings, opposite Cawood, severing the Cawood/York road. Four properties in Kelfield village were flooded.

Below Cawood, overflow into Cawood Marshes spread downstream into the Wistow Lordship and the northern outskirts of Selby, inundating an area of 1,370 ha, with about 15 million cu. m. of floodwater up to a maximum depth of 2.9 metres.

The village of Wistow was isolated with 12 properties flooded together with farmhouses in the Wistow Lordship.

In the Bondgate and northern areas of Selby, 118 houses suffered flooding to depths up to 1 metre and several commercial and industrial properties were affected.'

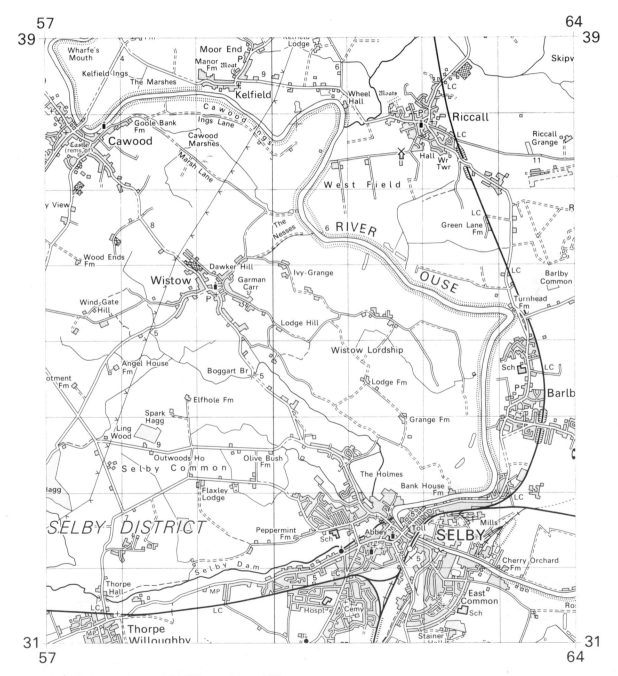

Figure 3.14 York Ordnance Survey 1:50,000 map (sheet 105)

| ACTIVITIES |

20 Trace Figure 3.15 which outlines the extent of
flooding in the Selby area. Place your tracing over
the map extract (Figure 3.14). Using the map and the
information on the York flood, answer the following:

   a What evidence is there on the map to suggest
     that flooding could be expected in this area?

   b Describe the types of land use in the areas
     affected by the floods.

   c With the aid of sketch maps, describe the
effects of the floods on: transport and
communications, settlements and individual
residents, farm land.

   d What scheme of flood protection already exists?
Would you recommend any other schemes?
Give reasons for your answer.

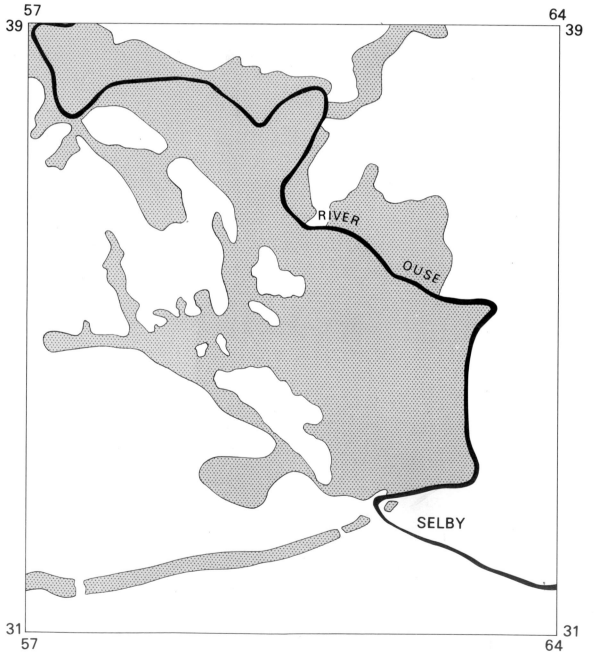

Figure 3.15 The York floods 1982

CHAPTER 4

Drought

What is drought?

Drought can be defined as a lack or shortage of water for an unusually long period of time. It can occur at any place in the world causing anything from mild annoyance at not being able to wash the car to death through famine. Some parts of the world have very little water anyway, so when the rains fail the effect can be disasterous; no drinking water, crops die, people starve. In other parts of the world, in industrial countries, droughts can cause water rationing and the closing down of industries.

A drought is a serious matter to the people affected in whichever part of the world, although it is important for us to realise that while we moan about dry games fields, in other parts of the world people are too weak because of starvation to even moan.

This chapter will examine experiences of drought in two different parts of the world – the Sahel area of Africa and the United Kingdom.

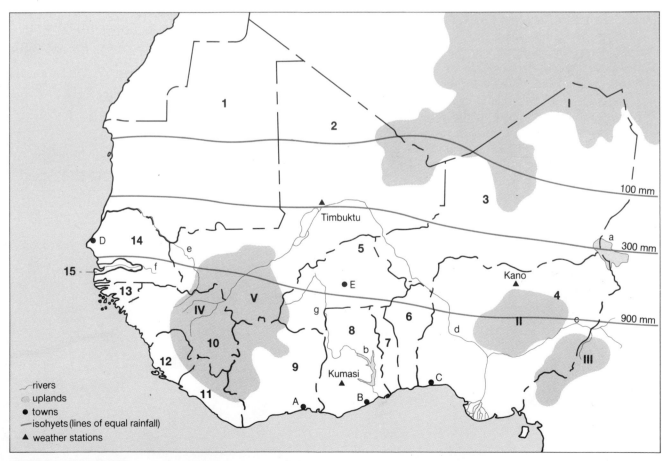

rivers
uplands
● towns
─ isohyets (lines of equal rainfall)
▲ weather stations

Figure 4.1 West Africa

ACTIVITIES

1 a Make a tracing of Figure 4.1 and use an atlas to
   label the following:
   countries   1–15,
   lakes   a and b,
   rivers   c–g,
   towns   A–E,
   uplands   I–V.
   If you use a key, make up suitable symbols.

 b The isohyets separate the regions of West
   Africa. Use colours to shade lightly the areas and
   label as following:
   north of 100 mm   **desert**   brown
   100 mm–300 mm   **sub-desert**   orange
   300 mm–900 mm   **Sahel**   yellow

The Developing World: The Sahel

One of the most renowned drought-affected areas
of the world is the Sahel in West Africa. The
Sahel is a belt about 500 kilometres wide at the
southern fringe of the Sahara Desert, stretching
from Senegal in the west to Chad in the east.

During the last 20 years the lack of water has
caused death and hardship to the people of the
Sahel area. During the drought of 1973–74 over
100,000 people died, mostly through starvation,
and millions of cattle perished. The situation has
become serious once more in the nineteen-
eighties as the continued lack of rainfall causes
widespread famine. Figure 4.2 shows very clearly
the tragedy of drought.

You will have seen in the press and on
television appeals from agencies such as Oxfam.

Figure 4.2 The tragedy of drought

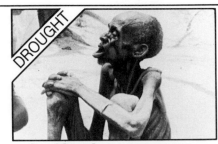

A little water never hurt anyone? It's killing him.

He's the victim of one of the most
crippling droughts on record. Many like him
have died, and now over a million people are
victims of the drought in Africa.

Your donation can help provide clean
water, food, medical equipment and other
essential supplies. It will bring relief to the
starving, it may prevent someone from dying.

Please help today, because for some,
tomorrow may be too late.

To: The Hon. Treasurer, The Rt. Hon. Lord Maybray-King, Help the Aged,
FREEPOST, London EC18 1BD. (no stamp needed)

I enclose my cheque/postal order for £ _____

Name (Mr/Mrs/Miss/Ms) _____

Address _____

_____ Postcode _____   **Help the Aged**

Figure 4.3 Help the Aged appeal

Figure 4.3 is one such appeal. The photograph highlights the basic lack of water for drinking. Many deaths, however, result from famine, for the lack of water means that crops do not grow and livestock have nothing on which to graze. The land becomes completely barren and the soil, baked by the sun, forms a hard surface which is impossible to plough.

In his book *Inside The Third World* Paul Harrison met a man called Moumouni Ouedraogo in Northern Burkina Faso (Upper Volta). Moumouni was a wrinkled 60 year old who lived with his four brothers and a total of nine wives and twenty-five children. They farmed the area around their living compound:

'Even close in to the compound, the soil looked poor enough, stony and dusty without a trace of humus (vegetation). And this was the only area that they ever fertilized, with the droppings of a donkey and a couple of goats. Outside a circle of about 50 yards diameter round the houses, the ground was a dark red, baked hard. It had been cultivated the year before but had yielded very little. Moumouni said that he didn't think anything would grow this year.'

One effect of drought is **migration** – the movement of people from place to place. When rural peasants are no longer able to obtain drinking water or food they move to areas where they hope to find plentiful supplies of both. In West Africa, this involves a general movement southwards to the wetter regions – regions often already overcrowded.

Bush fires may rage destroying the natural savanna grassland and any crops being grown. Although in the long term such fires provide soil nutrients, in the short term peasants are left without pasture land and crops. In 1983 the Ivory Coast lost 600,000 hectares of forest and plantation and 65 per cent of all crops due to a number of serious bush fires.

ACTIVITIES

2 Look back at Figure 4.2.
  a Describe the general landscape and vegetation.
  b What do you think the women are doing?
  c Why do you think there are no men in the photograph?
  d Imagine that this photograph was to be used for a newspaper appeal, much like Figure 4.3. Make up a headline.

3 The following account is another taken from Paul Harrison's book. Here Moumouni describes the rain that falls occasionally:

  'Before, it used to rain a lot but we didn't feel the hardness of the rain. Now it rains less, but the rain is getting harder and harder. The rain was not really harder. It "felt" harder because the exhausted soil was yielding less so there was less plant cover for the ground and nothing to break the rain's impact, beating down the soil and taking away the precious topsoil in sudden rivers formed out of nowhere.'

  a Much of the rain fall results from violent storms. How does the torrential rain cause further problems in farming the land?
  b If you were in Moumouni's position, what would you do to make more use of the water and try to prevent the problems arising from the heavy rainfall?

4 a Figure 4.4 shows a climate graph for Kew in London. Below is average climate data for three weather stations in West Africa. These are located for you on Figure 4.1. Draw graphs similar to the Kew graph using this data.

  b For all four graphs work out the following: average monthly temperature; temperature range (difference between highest and lowest); total annual rainfall.

  c Describe the main differences between the climates of Kew and West Africa.

  d How does the climate of West Africa change as one goes south?

		J	F	M	A	M	J	J	A	S	O	N	D
Timbuktu	temp (°C)	22	24	28	32	34	34	32	30	32	31	28	22
	rainfall (mm)	–	–	3	–	5	23	79	81	38	3	–	–
Kano	temp (°C)	21	24	28	31	31	28	26	25	26	27	24	22
	rainfall (mm)	–	–	3	10	69	117	206	310	142	13	–	–
Kumasi	temp (°C)	25	27	27	27	27	26	24	24	24	26	26	25
	rainfall (mm)	20	58	145	130	191	201	109	79	173	180	94	20

Causes

The drought and the associated famine in the Sahel are the combined result of the climate and of the activities of the people who live in the region. The climate is very different from our own.

As you will have discovered from Activity 4, West Africa has wet and dry seasons, as opposed to our hot (summer) and cold (winter) seasons. Rainfall, therefore, only occurs during a certain period of the year when it may even cause flooding! The situation is made worse by the fact that the high temperatures result in very rapid rates of evaporation. The overall result is a severe water shortage in the Sahel. The problem was made much worse between 1968 and 1974 when rainfall in the Sahel fell way below average.

The drought situation is made worse by man's own activities in the Sahel. By felling trees for firewood and house building and by poor farming causing for example, overgrazing, man is causing the deserts to spread; this process is called **desertification**. Land that used to be forest,

or even had settlements, has been transformed into rock and sand. It has been estimated that, on a world scale, an area the size of China has been turned into desert. The southern fringe of the Sahara is advancing southwards at an average of 10 kilometres per year.

This increase in desert serves to make the climate drier and so increases the drought risk. It also means that gradually less and less land is available to feed more and more people, so making famine much more likely during a drought period.

ACTIVITIES

5 Figure 4.5 shows a group of nomadic herders.
 a What are the different animals being herded?
 b For each type of animal try to suggest its value to the herders (hint: hides, milk).
 c How might these herders cause desertification?

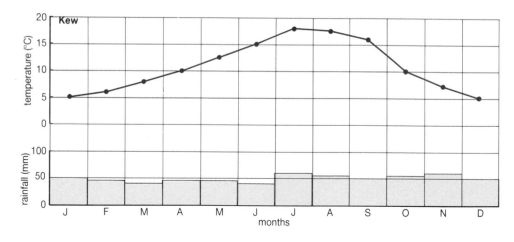

Figure 4.4 Climate graph for Kew, England

Figure 4.5 Nomadic herders in search of fresh pastures

How can the Sahelians cope with drought?

In a severe drought and famine, campaigns by agencies such as Oxfam, Help the Aged and the United Nations raise money for emergency aid. However important this may be at the time, it is not a long-term solution to the problem.

Water needs to be controlled and managed; it needs to be stored in the wet season for use during the long dry season. There are many water projects in the Sahel which can be divided into large scale and small scale:

1 Large scale projects These involve dams and reservoirs with many kilometres of canals for irrigating crops. One such project involves the cooperation of Senegal, Mali and Mauritania. Three dams are planned, at a cost of $1 billion (one thousand million), to provide a constant supply of water for farming, drinking and electricity production.

2 Small scale projects These involve the drilling of deep water wells, the installation of water pumps and the building of simple irrigation channels. Figure 4.7 shows a newly installed water well in Ethiopia. These schemes are of

Figure 4.6 A sea of fans fill Wembley Stadium for the Live Aid concert to aid starving Africans. The concert was viewed in 160 countries worldwide

Figure 4.7 A newly installed water well being checked by an Oxfam official

more value to the small villages and are much cheaper than the large scale projects. Over 1,500 boreholes have been sunk already in Mali, enabling small vegetable gardens to spring up in dusty little villages. The major problem with these wells is that water extraction causes the water table to drop and, as a result, the wells dry up! They need to be dug deeper and deeper.

One common small scale project is called **water harvesting**. This is where a number of small stone walls are built across a hillside to trap rainwater as it runs downhill. Normally the often-torrential rain simply flows as a sheet of water carrying the slope's topsoil with it. This type of project interrupts the flow, so giving the soil a chance to soak up the water.

Many of the charity agencies help in small scale projects. The 1983 Blue Peter Appeal, called 'Weather Beater', raised over £1 million for projects in the Third World. Some of this money is to be used to help the drought problem in the Sahel, for example, in Mauritania dykes, dams and wells are to be constructed.

Some countries have started a tree growing programme to try and stop the spread of the desert. For instance, in Mauritania volunteers go into the desert daily to plant and water young trees.

ACTIVITIES

6 Which type of project (large or small scale) do you think is best? Give reasons for your choice.

7 Study Figure 4.8(a) which shows a training officer illustrating the theory of water harvesting to local farmers in Burkina Faso.
   a Imagine that you are the training officer. What would you be saying to the local farmers?
   b Why is it important for the small walls or dykes to run *across* the slope, like contour lines, rather than *down* the slope?
   c Do you think training sessions such as the one shown are important? Explain your answer. Figure 4.8(b) shows the theory being turned into practice.
   d Why are the stones placed in a shallow trench?
   e Roughly how high is the wall?
   f Do you think that the area shown in Figure 4.8(a) needs this scheme? Give reasons for your reply.

Figure 4.8a Water harvesting – a training officer educating locals

b Water harvesting – practising the technique

Drought in the Developed World: England and Wales, 1976

In 1975/1976 England and Wales suffered its worst drought on record, although compared to the Sahel it was no more than a 'dry·spell'. No lives were lost, people did not starve and no large scale migration took place. However, a great deal of hardship was suffered by a modern industrial country that could have been brought to a standstill.

People throughout England and Wales had their water restricted. Some were not allowed to use hosepipes. Others had their water supply cut off for most of the day. In some areas standpipes in the street had to be used, as shown in Figure 4.9.

Industry as a whole suffered, as many industries use water for one purpose or another. For example, power stations use water for cooling. Steelworks, power stations and processing industries were very close to having to close by the time the rains eventually came in September 1976.

Probably the most serious effect was on

Figure 4.9 A standpipe in North Devon

agriculture Grass did not grow at all during the summer in most of Britain, leading to a shortage of milk. Canning and freezing factories had little to process and so bankruptcy threatened and food prices shot up. An estimated £500 million worth of crops were lost.

Figure 4.10 The dried-up River Thames

As the vegetation dried out so fires became a hazard. Forest fires in Wales destroyed hundreds of thousands of trees and in southern England heath fires broke out in many counties. In Dorset a forest fire spread rapidly towards a hospital causing over 300 people to be evacuated. Another effect of the fires was to destroy the natural habitats of rare flowers and birds.

Rivers were reduced to a trickle and some became completely dried up. Algae spread in the remaining water, absorbing all the oxygen and causing many fish to die through suffocation. Also, with less water to dilute pollutants, rivers became dangerous for swimmers and more expensive to treat. Figure 4.10 shows the River Thames during the height of the drought.

As the ground dried and cracked so house foundations became unstable and subsidence occurred. This problem was most severe in the South-East of England where many houses are built on clay which shrinks when it dries. It is estimated that £60 million worth of damage was caused to houses as a result of the drought.

The floor and sides of reservoirs also cracked as they dried, so that when they filled up eventually, a great deal of water leaked out through the cracks.

Figure 4.11 Water supply in Britain

ACTIVITIES

8 Use Figure 4.9 to help you describe some of the hardships suffered by people whose water supply was cut off during the summer of 1976.

9 Study Figure 4.10:
   a Describe the state of the River Thames.
   b Describe the effect on:
      water supply for domestic and industrial users;
      wildlife of the river and its banks;
      boating and leisure activities (fishing, walking, etc).

Causes

There are three types of water supply in Britain; reservoirs, rivers and groundwater (natural underground reservoirs). They are illustrated in Figure 4.11. The surface sources provide water for most of the country with groundwater being important in the South-East. Although groundwater levels dropped due to the lack of re-filling by rain, it was the surface sources that dried up most rapidly, due to the lack of rain and high rate of evapotranspiration. The gradual drying up of the water sources during 1975 and early 1976 led to the drought.

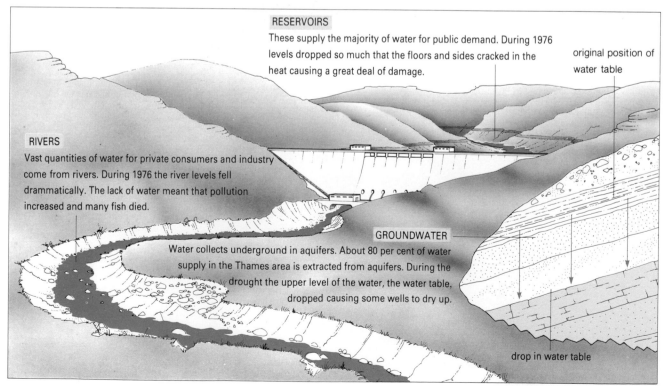

RESERVOIRS
These supply the majority of water for public demand. During 1976 levels dropped so much that the floors and sides cracked in the heat causing a great deal of damage.

original position of water table

RIVERS
Vast quantities of water for private consumers and industry come from rivers. During 1976 the river levels fell dramatically. The lack of water meant that pollution increased and many fish died.

GROUNDWATER
Water collects underground in aquifers. About 80 per cent of water supply in the Thames area is extracted from aquifers. During the drought the upper level of the water, the water table, dropped causing some wells to dry up.

drop in water table

ACTIVITIES

10 Study Figures 4.12, 4.13 and 4.14 which show rainfall, July temperatures and the distribution of population. Use the maps to answers the following questions.

a Which parts of the country receive, on average:
the most rainfall?
the least rainfall?

b Which parts of the country have the highest July temperatures and, as a result, the highest rates of evaporation?

c Which parts of the country would you expect to be most at risk from drought? Explain your answer.

So why did the water sources dry up? As you have discovered from Activity 10, certain parts of the country are at risk from drought. The risk became reality when rainfall remained below average for about fifteen months, from May 1975. Temperatures of over 30°C during June, July and August 1976 caused rapid evaporation of surface water.

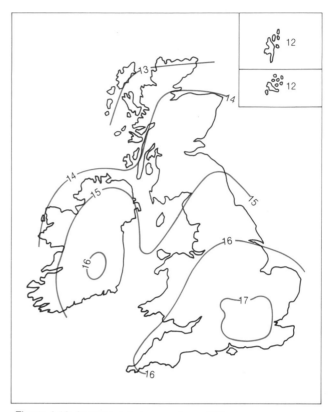

Figure 4.13 Average July temperatures (°C)

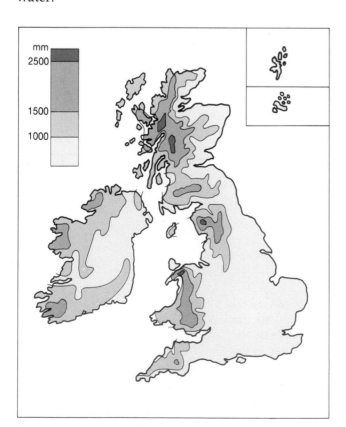

Figure 4.12 Mean annual precipitation

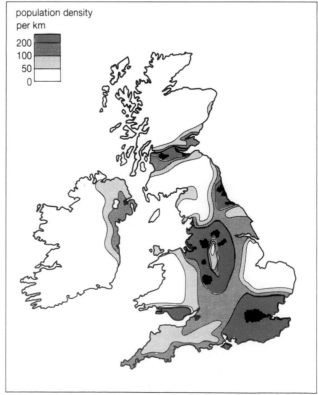

Figure 4.14 Population distribution

ACTIVITIES

11 a Copy Figure 4.15, completing the column showing the difference between the actual monthly rainfall and the average monthly rainfall. To help you the first three entries have been done.

b Draw a bar graph, like Figure 4.16, to show whether the monthly figures were above or below average. Again the first three entries have been done for you. Use different colours for above and below averages.

c For how many months was the rainfall below average?

d Work out the difference between the total amount of actual rainfall and the total amount of average rainfall for the twelve months from September 1975 to August 1976.

Date	Actual rainfall (mm)	Average rainfall (1916–1950) (mm)	Difference between actual and average rainfall (mm)
Oct 1974	99	92	+7
Nov 1974	125	95	+30
Dec 1974	72	88	−16
Jan 1975	117	92	
Feb 1975	31	66	
Mar 1975	81	57	
Apr 1975	71	60	
May 1975	47	63	
Jun 1975	21	55	
Jul 1975	66	79	
Aug 1975	52	81	
Sep 1975	107	76	
Oct 1975	36	92	
Nov 1975	73	95	
Dec 1975	50	88	
Jan 1976	60	92	
Feb 1976	40	66	
Mar 1976	43	57	
Apr 1976	21	60	
May 1976	64	63	
Jun 1976	17	55	
Jul 1976	32	79	
Aug 1976	27	81	
Sep 1976	160	76	

Figure 4.15 Rainfall figures for England and Wales

The problem was made worse by a number of other factors:

1 a huge increase in demand for water during the 1960s and 1970s, especially from industry;

2 the wastage of water by all users; water was thought to be limitless and was taken for granted;

3 leaks from old reservoirs and pipes, accounting for one-fifth of the water 'used'.

How did Britain cope with the drought?

During the drought the main policy adopted was to conserve the remaining stocks of water by reducing the demand. All users were encouraged to **save water**! Both the Water Authorities and the Government ran a huge publicity campaign involving posters, badges and radio jingles. In Devon a 10 metre long SAVE WATER streamer was towed behind a power boat along the most popular beaches! On 6 August the Drought Act came into force and a Drought Minister was appointed to coordinate water saving policies. Typically, soon after it rained! The Act gave the ten Water Authorities in England and Wales the power to restrict water to customers. Many authorities banned the use of water for the following activities:

1 watering of parks, gardens, lawns, sports grounds, golf courses, race courses;

2 filling of private swimming pools and ornamental ponds;

3 washing of road vehicles;

4 cleaning of exteriors of buildings.

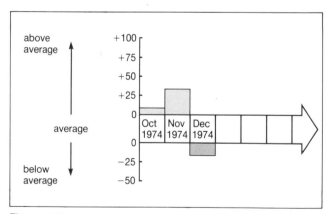

Figure 4.16

Demand needs to be reduced and supply increased so that we are better prepared for long, dry spells in the future. Consumers must realize that water is not limitless, but that it is precious and must be used sparingly. Supply is being increased by the building of new reservoirs and there is a plan for a national water grid along the same lines as the electricity national grid. Figure 4.17 shows the proposed plan. New reservoirs in

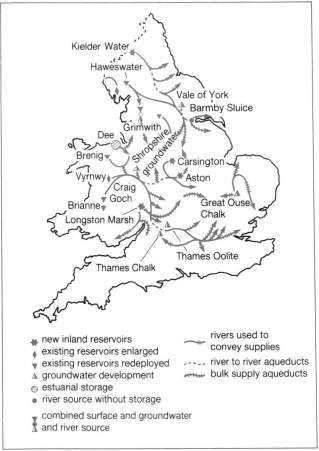

Figure 4.17 The national water grid

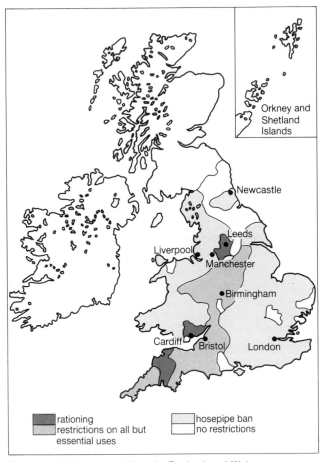

Figure 4.18 Water restrictions in England and Wales

the north and west will be able to supply the drier parts of the country by linking up with rivers using aquaducts. The original scheme has been shelved although individual projects have been started. The cost of the scheme would be about £6 billion!

ACTIVITIES

12 Design a poster, badge or jingle to encourage people to save water.

13 Figure 4.18 shows the water restrictions at the height of the drought.
   a Estimate the proportion of the country affected by:
      the hosepipe ban;
      the restriction on all but 'essential uses';
      the rationing.
   b What do you think is meant by 'essential uses'?
   c Which parts of England and Wales had water rationing?
   d Give possible reasons why South-East England was not so affected by the drought as those areas listed in c.

14 Figure 4.17 shows the proposed national water grid.
   a Copy the map and use colours to highlight its features more clearly.
   b Why is water to be moved, in general, from the north and west to the south and east? (Refer back to Activity 10 for help.)
   c How many new reservoirs would be built?
   d How many reservoirs would be enlarged?
   e How many groundwater sites would be developed?
   f How would water move from the River Severn to the River Thames?
   g What do you think is meant by the 'estuarial storage' planned for the River Dee?

CHAPTER 5

Strong winds

Introduction

This chapter will describe the causes and effects of strong winds. It will examine the power and destruction of hurricanes and tornadoes as well as the problem of gales in Britain. However, before this it is important to understand what wind is and how it is measured.

What is wind?

Wind is the invisible movement of air from one place to another. It is caused by differences in atmospheric pressure and can be easily understood by thinking of a bicycle tyre. If the tyre valve is undone, air rushes out; this is wind! It moves from the tyre, where the pressure is high, into the open, where pressure is relatively low. When the pressure inside the tyre is equal to the pressure outside, no more air passes out; the wind stops.

In the atmosphere there are many differences in pressure causing air to circulate. In Britain we are concerned with small (on a world scale) areas of high pressure (**anticyclones**) and areas of low pressure (**depressions** or **cyclones**). Air moves from anticyclones to depressions – high to low pressure.

The strength of the wind depends on the difference in pressure between two points; the greater the difference in pressure, the greater the wind speed.

Atmospheric pressure is measured in millibars (mb). On a weather map points of equal pressure are joined by lines called **isobars**. These are usually drawn at intervals of 4 mb. If there are a lot of closely spaced isobars then the pressure difference between two points will be great and the wind strong. Therefore, a good rule to remember is: **the closer the isobars, the stronger the wind**!

Wind speed can be described using the Beaufort Scale, devised by Admiral Beaufort at the beginning of the nineteenth century. There

ACTIVITIES

1 Figure 5.1 is weather map of Britain. The details of the weather are recorded at a number of weather stations. Notice how symbols are used rather than writing; the symbols are explained in the key. Notice also the isobars crossing the map. The numbers are the pressure readings in millibars. Study the map and key carefully:

  a Are the winds strongest in England, Wales or Scotland? How do you know this?

b For each of the weather stations, A-F, describe the weather by completing the table below:

c Draw weather symbols for three stations with weather conditions as follows:

  1 cloud 8 oktas, temperature 3°C, drizzle, wind 3–7 knots westerly;

  2 cloud 3 oktas, temperature 22°C, rain shower, wind 1–2 knots southerly;

  3 cloud 8 oktas, temperature 16°C, thunderstorm, wind 18–22 knots easterly.

station	temp (°C)	cloud cover	wind speed	wind direction	weather
A Southampton					
B Western Ireland					
C Peterhead					
D Manchester					
E Norfolk					
F Exeter					

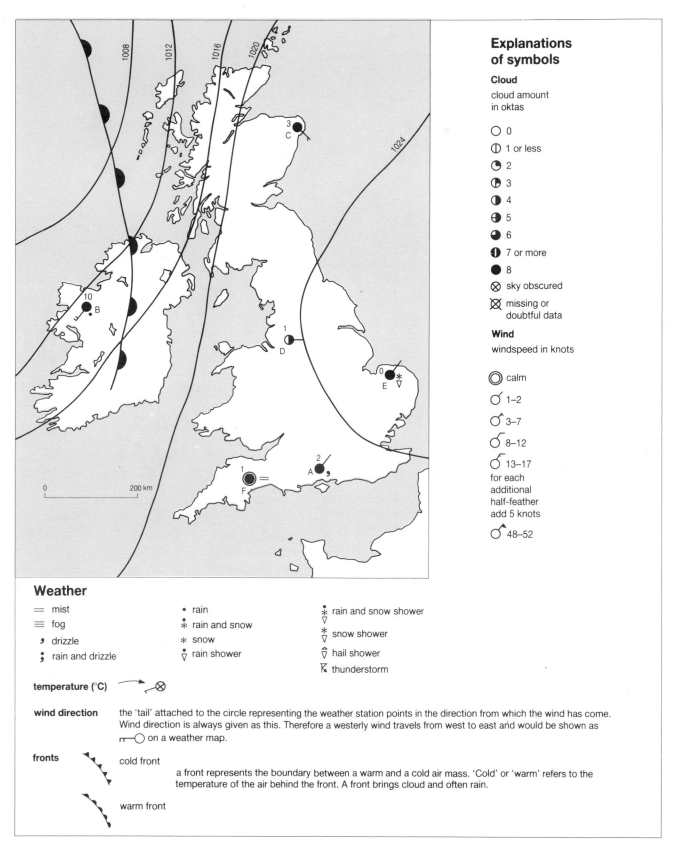

Figure 5.1 Weather map 5 February

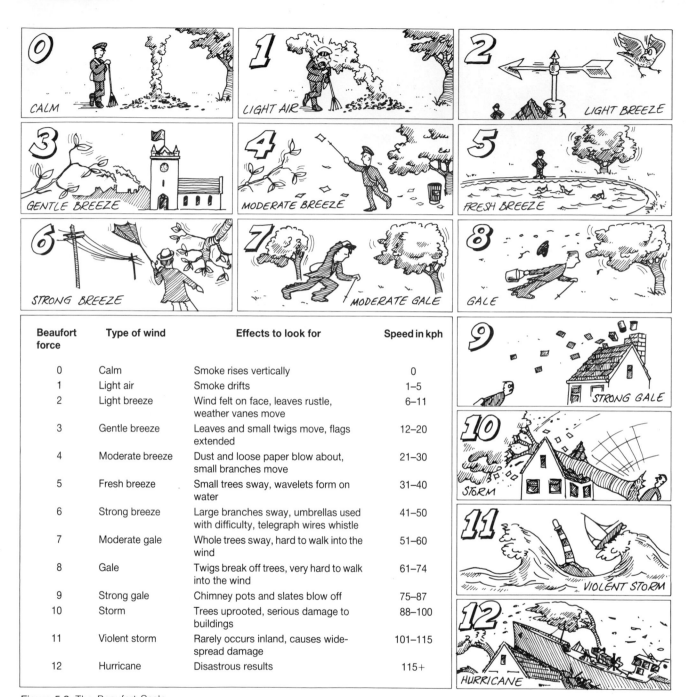

Figure 5.2 The Beaufort Scale

Beaufort force	Type of wind	Effects to look for	Speed in kph
0	Calm	Smoke rises vertically	0
1	Light air	Smoke drifts	1–5
2	Light breeze	Wind felt on face, leaves rustle, weather vanes move	6–11
3	Gentle breeze	Leaves and small twigs move, flags extended	12–20
4	Moderate breeze	Dust and loose paper blow about, small branches move	21–30
5	Fresh breeze	Small trees sway, wavelets form on water	31–40
6	Strong breeze	Large branches sway, umbrellas used with difficulty, telegraph wires whistle	41–50
7	Moderate gale	Whole trees sway, hard to walk into the wind	51–60
8	Gale	Twigs break off trees, very hard to walk into the wind	61–74
9	Strong gale	Chimney pots and slates blow off	75–87
10	Storm	Trees uprooted, serious damage to buildings	88–100
11	Violent storm	Rarely occurs inland, causes wide-spread damage	101–115
12	Hurricane	Disastrous results	115+

ACTIVITIES

2 Make a sketch of Figure 5.3. Use the text to help you label your sketch.

3 Which of the two methods of measurement (anemometer and Beaufort Scale) do you think is most widely used? Explain your answer.

4 Make a daily note of the wind speed at your home or school for a fortnight, using the Beaufort Scale. Draw a bar graph like the one in Figure 5.4 using your observations. Try to record during two different seasons to see if there is any difference.

Figure 5.3 An anemometer

What is a hurricane?

Figure 5.5 A hurricane viewed from space off the west of the USA

are 12 points, or 'forces', on the scale, each one referring to a particular effect. Figure 5.2 shows this scale. As you can see, wind only becomes a hazard when it reaches gale force or above.

Wind is measured with an **anemometer** (Figure 5.3). This consists of four cups connected to a central pivot which rotates. The rotation operates a meter which shows the speed either in miles per hour (as in Figure 5.2) or in **knots**.

One knot = 1 nautical mile per hour = 1.15 miles per hour = 1.86 kilometres per hour.

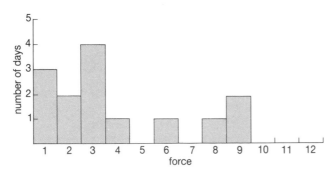

Figure 5.4

A hurricane is a severe tropical storm or cyclone. In the Far East it is called a **typhoon**. Figure 5.5 is a hurricane photographed from space.

This swirling mass of cloud may cover an area of 160 square km and move at a speed of 80 km per hour. It brings very strong winds, which may reach 320 km per hour, and heavy rain. Hurricanes are summer storms and are found in low latitudes.

What is the hurricane hazard?

Hurricanes have three major effects: strong winds, heavy rain and storm surges. The winds cause damage to property by lifting roofs, for example. Caravans may be picked up and rolled or bounced many metres before coming to rest on their sides or roofs. Posts and metal sheets may be whisked up, becoming an obvious danger, and fields of crops may be flattened completely.

Figure 5.6 Storm surge from Hurricane Camille, 1948; the south coast of the USA

Torrential rain may produce 150–300 centimetres of rain in a single day, which can result in flooding as rivers overflow their banks. Hurricane Diane led to the drowning of 200 people in the United States in 1955.

The greatest hazard is a storm surge. This is a rapid rise in sea level resulting from the moving hurricane. A wall of water some 25 metres high can demolish houses and harbours and drown many people. Surges are thought to cause 90 per cent of deaths resulting from hurricanes. Figure 5.6 shows a storm surge caused by a hurricane. Notice the high battering waves.

Hurricanes are serious hazards. They cause loss of life and injury, destruction of crops and property, as well as creating terror and worry in those affected by them.

ACTIVITIES

5 Study Figure 5.7.
  a Use the scale to work out how high the normal high tide is above mean sea level. Remember to measure vertical height!
  b During a hurricane storm surge:
    how high above mean sea level is the storm surge?
    how high above normal high tide is the storm surge?

6 Copy each diagram in Figure 5.7. Describe what is happening in each one.

7 Figure 5.8 is a photograph of Miami Beach following a serious hurricane in October 1950. Describe the effects of the hurricane and try to think of the problems caused by the destruction.

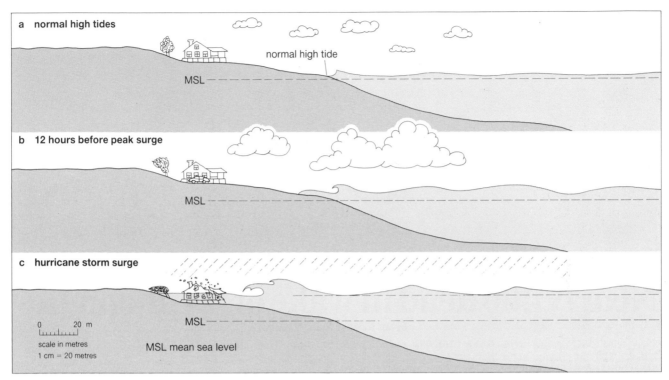

a normal high tides

normal high tide

MSL

b 12 hours before peak surge

MSL

c hurricane storm surge

MSL

0   20 m

scale in metres
1 cm = 20 metres

MSL mean sea level

Figure 5.7 The effects of a typical hurricane storm surge

Figure 5.8 Damage to Miami, USA following a hurricane in 1950

Storm victim: Waves smashing an inter-island vessel against the shore in Cebu during the height of the typhoon.

Nearly 400 dead in wake of Typhoon Ike

From Keith Dalton, Manila

At least 381 people were killed, 200 of them at a devastated lakeside town during Sunday's destructive rampage of Typhoon Ike through the Southern Philippines, officials said yesterday.

Provincial authorities in Surigao del Norte, on the north-eastern tip of Mindanao Island, said most of the 200 victims in Mainit town drowned when 137 mph winds churned up lake waters which smashed down houses dotted along the shoreline.

Another 82 people died in the provincial capital Surigao 30 miles away, where journalists reported that the majority of buildings were badly damaged. As many as 1,000 people may have perished in the province. About 340 people were injured and dozens were missing.

The typhoon tore a 300-mile-wide path of destruction through the whole region.

About 160,000 people were homeless.

The reporters arrived in Surigao on board an Air Force plane carrying 35,000lb of emergency food and medical supplies after the city mayor, Mr Constantino Navarro, radioed for urgent assistance.

Rescue workers on Nonoc Island nearby reported 35 people dead, and 18 more fatalities in three other provinces were announced.

President Marcos in an emergency early morning meeting with senior government and military advisers, added Surigao, Iloilo and Palawan provinces to 21 others proclaimed as calamity zones last Thursday after tropical storm Jane left 53 people dead and tens of thousands homeless.

Almost the entire central Visayas region was blacked out after Typhoon Ike tore down both power and communica-

tion lines. Long after Ike had moved out to sea the National Disaster Coordination Centre set up in army headquarters had still not received any reports of destruction or casualty figures from many densely populated islands hit by the typhoon.

Until full communications are restored the full extent of destruction, loss of life and the number of people made homeless cannot be accurately gauged.

● SEOUL: About 2,000 angry flood victims beat up several policemen yesterday as they stormed district offices accusing officials of negligence for failing to take proper flood prevention measures (AFP reports).

The Home Ministry's disaster centre reported 86 people dead, 40 missing, presumed drowned, and 89 injured in South Korea's worst rainstorms in 12 years. It esti-

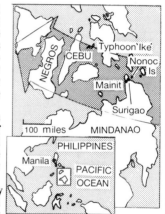

mated flood damage at £13m.

The demonstrations came soon after flood waters began to subside and an estimated 80,000 people who had been forced out of their homes were able to return to assess damage.

The Times, 4 September 1984

Figure 5.9 The effects of Typhoon Ike, March 1984

	Japan	USA	Scotland	Australia	Cuba*	Bangladesh*	India*	Haiti*	Mexico*	Honduras*
Total number of deaths	5,403	675	20	60	3,500	1,090,130	120,000	4,250	965	8,000
Number of major storms	3	12	1	2	1	8	2	2	3	1
Average deaths per storm										

Figure 5.10 Details of deaths caused by major storms 1959–75

ACTIVITIES

8 Read through the newspaper article of Figure 5.9 which describes the effects of Hurricane Ike.

a Copy the map to show the path of the typhoon (hurricane).

b Make a detailed list of the damage caused by the typhoon.

c Which of the following hurricane characteristics do you think caused the most deaths?: strong winds, heavy rain, storm surge. Explain your decision.

8 d Why were casualty figures slow in reaching the National Disaster Coordination Centre? Might you expect the death toll to rise still further even after Hurricane Ike has passed? Why?

9 a Make a copy of Figure 5.10. Complete the table.

b The countries with an asterisk (*) are **developing** countries. Do they appear to suffer more than the developed countries? Why do you think this is?

Your answer to Activity 9b may be correct, but an accurate answer can be achieved by applying Spearman's Rank Correlation Test to the problem. This is a statistical method of testing the relationship, or correlation, between two characteristics, in this case the 'average deaths per storm' and the 'development' of a country. The wealth of a country can be taken to represent its 'development.' Wealth is measured by Gross National product (GNP), which is the total value of goods and services produced by a country per capita (per person).

10 To carry out Spearman's Rank Correlation Test, copy the table below and follow each stage carefully:

a Complete column 3 by ranking the countries in descending order for the factor given in column 2. Bangladesh has the highest number of deaths so it is ranked number 1; India the next highest, so it is number 2; and so on.

b Complete column 5 by ranking the countries in order for the factor given in column 4. The first three entries have been done for you.

c Complete column 6 by working out the difference (d) between each country's ranks. For example, if a country ranked 6 in column 3 and 3 in column 5, the difference would be 3.

d Complete column 7 by squaring the differences to give you d².

e Add up the differences squared (d²) to discover Σd^2 (Σ means 'the sum of').

10 f Insert Σd^2 into the following formula:

$$R = 1 - \frac{(6 \times \Sigma d^2)}{(n^3 - n)}$$

R = Spearman's Rank
n = number of countries (10 in this case)

g You will end up with a value for R lying between +1 and −1. If your value is positive (+) this tells you than the relationship is positive, that is, that as one factor increases, so does the other; if your value is negative (−) this tells you that the relationship is negative, that is, that as one factor increases, so the other decreases. A value of +1 or −1 indicates a **perfect** relationship. A value between 0.7 (+ or −) and 1 (+ or −) indicates a **strong** relationship. A value below 0.7 indicates a weak relationship, the nearer to 0 the weaker it is.

h Write down your value for R and explain its meaning.

i Does it support your statement in Activity 9b?

1 country	2 average deaths per major tropical storm 1959–1977	3 rank (of column 2)	4 GNP per head (US dollars) 1974	5 rank (of column 4)	6 difference between columns 3 and 5 (d)	7 difference squared (d²)
Bangladesh*	136,266	1	70			
India*	60,000	2	110			
Honduras*	8,000	3	320			
Cuba*	3,500		510			
Haiti*	2,125		130			
Japan	1,801		1,920			
Mexico*	321		670			
USA	56		4,760	1		
Australia	30		2,980	2		
Scotland	20		2,270	3		
						$\Sigma d^2 =$

Bangladesh (1970)

On 12 November 1970 at about 11 p.m. a severe hurricane struck the lowlying coast of Bangladesh (see Figure 5.11). It brought with it a storm surge of about 7 metres above normal high tide, which swept over 26,000 square kilometres. By the morning of the 13th at least 225,000 people were dead, 280,000 cattle drowned, $63 million worth of crops destroyed and 2.5 million people left homeless. Being a poor country there was not enough food or shelter and the lack of medical help meant that the death toll rose rapidly to between 1 and 2 million people as starvation and disease took a hold.

Local newspaper reporters described the scene:

'Bodies which could not be buried have started decomposing. The air is filled with a bad smell and the small number of survivors are without food. I saw about 800 bodies lying on both sides of the dam badly damaged by the tidal wave.'

'I saw at least 3,000 bodies littered along the road. Survivors wandered like mad people crying out the names of their dead ones. There were 5,000 bodies in graves, 100–150 in each grave.'

This is one of the world's worst natural disasters, although it is not the only time that the Bay of Bengal has suffered, for in 1737 a 12 metre storm surge killed an estimated 300,000 people. In 1985 Bangladesh was hit again.

Caribbean and USA (1980)

During August 1980 Hurricane Allen passed through the Caribbean, causing death and a great deal of damage (Figure 5.12). It was tracked all the way by radar and 'planes so that warnings could be issued to countries liable to be in its path.

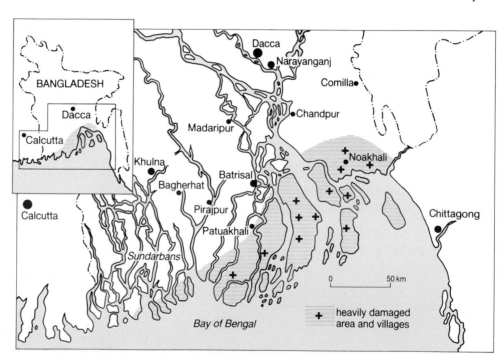

Figure 5.11 The Bangladesh Hurricane, 1970

Country/area	Strong winds	Heavy rain	Storm surge	Deaths	Effects Houses damaged	Other effects	Cost (millions of dollars)
Barbados	✓				500	n/a	1.5
St Lucia	✓	✓		18	n/a	n/a	n/a
Haiti	✓	✓		220	100,000+	half total coffee crop destroyed	400
Jamaica	✓	✓		8	n/a	n/a	n/a
Cayman Island/Cuba	✓			3	large number	n/a	n/a
Texas, USA	✓	✓	✓	24	n/a	oil platforms collapsed, 500,000 evacuated	600

n/a: information not available.

Figure 5.12 The effects of Hurricane Allen, August 1980

Figure 5.13 Hurricane tracking chart

Date	Time (GMT)	Position Latitude	Position Longitude	Pressure (MB)	Wind (knots)
	1200	12.8	55.6	975	80
	1800	12.9	57.5	965	95
4/8	0000	13.3	59.1	950	110
	0600	13.6	61.0	948	115
	1200	14.0	63.0	945	125
	1800	14.4	64.9	930	130
5/8	0000	14.8	66.7	911	140
	0600	15.4	68.6	916	145
	1200	15.9	70.5	932	155
	1800	16.5	72.3	940	150
6/8	0000	17.8	73.8	945	140
	0600	18.3	75.9	955	115
	1200	19.2	78.0	955	115
	1800	20.0	80.1	955	125
7/8	0000	20.1	81.9	945	135
	0600	20.4	83.6	935	145
	1200	21.0	84.8	910	155
	1800	21.8	86.4	899	165
8/8	0000	22.2	87.9	920	155
	0600	22.8	89.2	945	130
	1200	23.4	90.5	960	115
	1800	23.9	91.8	940	130
9/8	0000	24.5	93.0	912	145
	0600	25.0	94.2	909	155
	1200	25.2	95.4	916	140
	1800	25.4	96.1	925	125
10/8	0000	25.8	96.8	935	110
	0600	26.1	97.2	945	100
	1200	26.7	98.1	960	85
	1800	27.3	99.0	970	70

Figure 5.14 Positions of Hurricane Allen, 3 August–10 August 1980

ACTIVITIES

11 Plot the course of Hurricane Allen.

a Lay a sheet of tracing paper over Figure 5.13 and draw the outline of the USA, Central and South America, and the islands of the Caribbean.

b Plot carefully the course of the hurricane using the 6-hourly positions given in Figure 5.14. Notice that the first part of the course has been done for you. In order to show the full extent of the 250 kilometre wide storm, two parallel lines have been drawn 125 kilometres (0.5 centimetres) either side of the central line. As you continue to plot the course always make sure that the 'line' is 250 kilometres (1 centimetre) thick.

c When plotting is finished, lightly shade the course taken by the hurricane.

d Which countries suffered the full force of the hurricane?

e Work out the average speed of the hurricane (in kilometres per hour) as it moved between St Lucia (0600 hours on 4 August) and Jamaica (0600 hours on 6 August). To do this, work out the total distance in kilometres and divide by the total time taken in hours.

12 a Why do you think Bangladesh suffered much more loss of life than the USA and the Caribbean?

b Why do you think the USA and the Caribbean suffered much more financial loss than Bangladesh?

How are hurricanes caused?

A hurricane is one of the most powerful natural hazards on Earth. It releases energy equal to the explosion of a hydrogen bomb every minute of its existence. This vast amount of energy is obtained from heat and moisture, so the ideal location for a hurricane to form is over an ocean somewhere near the Equator.

Firstly, a core of moist warm air rises (warm air rises like steam from a kettle) and as it does so it cools and condenses to form water droplets and clouds. Air near the surfaces rushes into the space left by the rising pocket of air and, due to the rotation of the Earth, the hurricane begins to revolve, so adopting the typical spiral or Catherinewheel shape. (Look back at Figure 5.5.) The spiral with its strong winds and heavy rain moves with the prevailing winds across the world from east to west.

A fully mature hurricane may be hundreds of kilometres in diameter. In the centre is an area of calm, dry and sunny weather called the **eye**. After a period of severe weather the eye represents a welcome break of about half an hour before a repeat dose of strong winds and rain.

In order for a hurricane to survive it needs constant fuelling with energy; if its supply is cut off the hurricane will fade and die.

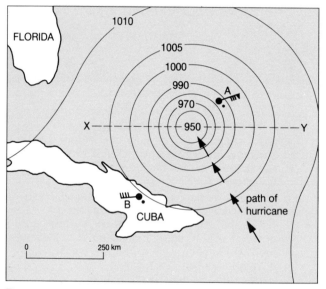

Figure 5.15 Weather map of a hurricane in the West Indies

ACTIVITIES

13 a Study Figure 5.15. Is it a hurricane, a depression, or an anticyclone? Explain your answer.

   b Refer to Figure 5.17. Where is the source area of this hurricane?

   c If you take the outer edge of the hurricane as being the 1,005 isobar, use the scale to work out its diameter.

   d Describe the weather conditions at:
   A, in the main body of the storm
   B, on the island of Cuba.

14 Figure 5.16 is a cross-section along the line X–Y of Figure 5.15. Make a copy of the cross-section, adding the following labels:
   1 rapid rising air forming cloud
   2 heavy rainfall and strong winds
   3 outer area of cloud and lighter rain
   4 'eye' formed by gently falling air.

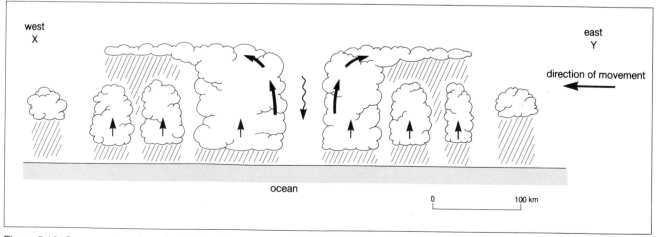

Figure 5.16 Cross section along line X–Y on Figure 5.15

ACTIVITIES

15 Figure 5.17 shows the main hurricane source areas and the main paths taken by hurricanes.

a On a world outline draw carefully the eight areas.

b The eight areas are listed below. Use an atlas to identify and label each area.

  1 Arafura Sea (northern Australia)
  2 West Indies
  3 South Pacific Islands (Fiji)
  4 Eastern Pacific (Off Central America)
  5 Western Pacific (Off Japan)
  6 Central Indian Ocean
  7 Arabian Sea
  8 North Indian Ocean (Off Sumatra)

c Mark the ten countries severely affected by hurricanes (Activity 9).

d For each country name the likely source area(s) for its hurricanes.

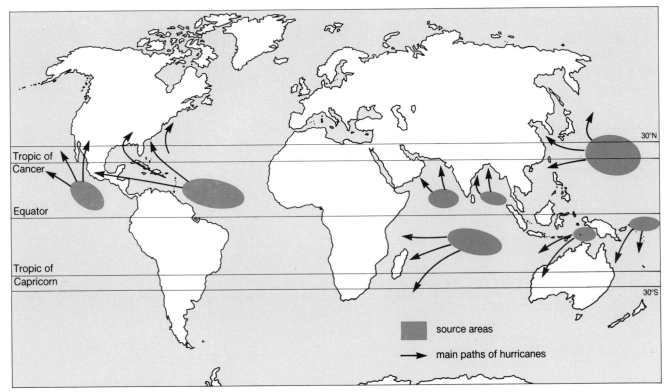

Figure 5.17 Hurricane source areas and paths

Can the hurricane hazard be reduced?

For most of the countries affected by hurricanes there is little that can be done to reduce the destruction of property and the flattening of crops. This is because they are poor Third World countries, without the technology to predict the storms or the money to compensate people for their losses.

In the wealthier countries, such as the USA, hurricanes can be detected and plotted by radar, so that warnings can be given to the public well in advance. Members of the public can plot a hurricane's course, as you did in Activity 11. Coastal areas can be strengthened against surges by the building of sea walls and shutters over windows will protect against strong winds. The Americans have also tried 'cloud seeding'. Dry ice (solid carbon dioxide) is released into clouds to cause rainfall and drain off some of the energy of the hurricane. Unfortunately this technique has not been very successful. Indeed in 1947 a harmless hurricane suddenly doubled back after 'seeding', causing the state of Georgia much damage!

Hurricane protection in Miami, Florida, USA

Miami is one of the wealthiest American tourist centres, but it suffers hurricanes, on average one every 7 years. Miami Beach is a 15 kilometre sand bar with many hotels and high class housing areas. However, nowhere is the land higher than 3.5 metres above sea level. A severe surge could completely flood Miami Beach.

Due to the serious nature of this problem, over 64 million dollars is being spent to make Miami 'hurricane-proof'.

Figure 5.18 shows the protection schemes. Careful evacuation routes have been planned, as shown by the arrows. The beach itself has been widened to create a buffer zone, to reduce the effect of a storm surge, and all new buildings have been built on artificial mounds 6 metres above sea level.

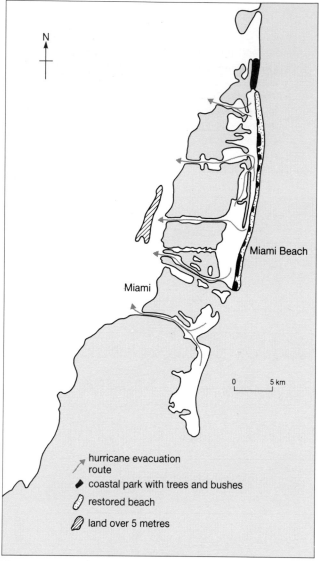

Figure 5.18 Hurricane protection in Miami, Florida

ACTIVITIES

16 a Explain in your own words why Miami Beach could suffer greatly during a hurricane.

b What do you think is the reason for having a number of parks with trees and bushes at intervals along the beach?

c Describe how the following facts might cause evacuation difficulties.
45 per cent of Miami Beach's population is over 60 years old and 8 per cent are described as frail; the only means of evacuation is by five long and narrow bridges.

d The low-lying land of Miami Beach is similar to the islands of Bangladesh (Figure 5.11). Would you expect to find similar protection schemes in operation in that country? Explain your answer.

Tornadoes

Photograph Figure 5.19 is instantly recognizable as a tornado or 'twister', as it is called in America. Tornadoes are the most powerful storms, although their funnel-like shapes mean that they affect only small surface areas, 100–500 metres in diameter. They move at speeds up to 80 km per hour, carving destructive paths through landscapes.

Tornadoes are known for their strong winds (up to 800 km per hour) and severe updraughts, which act like huge vacuum cleaners, able to suck clothes off people and feathers off chickens!

They can lift cars, people and even houses. In Minnesota, USA, in 1931, a tornado lifted an 85 tonne railway carriage with 117 passengers inside it 25 metres off the ground!

For those directly in the path of a tornado the experience can be terrifying, as the following account makes clear:

'I opened the door and saw a great wall that seemed to be smoke, driving in front of it white billows that looked like steam. There was a deep roar, like a train, but many, many times louder. The air was full of

Figure 5.19 Tornado in Jasper, Minnesota, USA

everything – boards, branches of trees, pans, stoves all churning around together. I saw whole sides of houses rolling along near the ground. Then the storm hit me. I was blown back into the restaurant and against the stove. The building rocked back and forth and then it began to fall in. Fire flashed in great puffs from the stove.'

Tornadoes do not move in straight lines but twist and turn and even double back, so making their paths impossible to predict.

They do not usually last for more than a few kilometres although there have been exceptions. For example, in 1925 a tornado cut its way through the Mid-West of the USA for 350 kilometres killing 670 people.

Tornadoes are found in many parts of the world but are very common in the central states of the USA during the summer months when up

Figure 5.20 An approaching tornado

ACTIVITIES

17 Use the account to help you list some of the effects and damage that may result from a passing tornado.

18 Figure 5.20 shows a tornado. Imagine that it was to move down the street on the photograph. Describe the likely effects of the tornado on this particular street.

Figure 5.21 Stages in the formation of a tornado during May 1970, Kansas, USA

ACTIVITIES

19 Figure 5.21 shows a tornado gradually forming. Make a sketch of each photograph and describe what is happening.

to 1,000 may be reported every year. Their formation is uncertain although they result from sudden and very rapid rises of hot air; why small pockets of air should rise suddenly is not clearly understood.

They cannot be prevented from forming. The only way to cope with them is to take shelter in a basement. As they are sudden events, prediction is very difficult.

Strong winds in Britain

Britain is battered frequently by strong winds which commonly reach Force 8 or above on the Beaufort Scale. Gales are most common in the uplands and the west of Britain as they bear the brunt of the prevailing westerly winds which come off the Atlantic.

The strong winds can damage houses. In fact, on average 230,000 buildings in Britain are damaged every year, although most lose only a few roof slates. People are killed by falling debris and trees and a few are literally blown off mountain tops and sea cliffs annually. In gales during January 1976 28 people were killed and damage worth £1 million was caused.

Figure 5.22 Effects of strong winds in Britain

a

b

c

Tornadoes are by no means rare in Britain. There are more tornadoes per square kilometre in Britain than in the USA, although they are not as powerful usually. One of the most serious tornadoes of recent times hit Newmarket on 3 January 1978. It carved a path 200 metres wide through the town lifting cars and even shifting a railway signal box off its foundations.

Tornadoes in Britain tend to occur during very severe weather in winter. A typical cause would be a fast moving severe depression (area of low pressure) moving across the country.

ACTIVITIES

21 Figure 5.23 gives the location and times of tornadoes that occurred in England and Wales as a severe depression crossed the country on 23 November 1981.

a Use an atlas to help you plot the twenty-one tornadoes on an outline map of England and Wales. In order to show the different times a colour key could be used, as follows:

10.01–11.00 hours	yellow
11.01–12.00 hours	orange
12.01–13.00 hours	red
13.01–14.00 hours	light brown
14.01–15.00 hours	dark brown
15.01–16.00 hours	black

Mark each location with a cross of the correct colour.

b Use your map to suggest the course of the severe depression.

Figure 5.23 Tornadoes in England and Wales on 23 November 1981

Location	Time
Holyhead (Gwynedd)	10.34
Wallasey (Merseyside)	11.30
St Helens (Merseyside)	11.50
Kenilworth (Warwickshire)	12.00
Market Drayton (Shropshire)	12.00
Oldham (Greater Manchester)	12.00
Warrington (Cheshire)	12.00
Wem (Shropshire)	12.05
Hull (Humberside)	13.30
Stoneleigh, near Leamington (Warwickshire)	14.00
Higham Ferrers (Northamptonshire)	14.20

Location	Time
Wellingborough (Northamptonshire)	14.20
Caldecott, near Corby (Leicestershire)	14.30
Flitwick, near Ampthill (Bedfordshire)	14.30
Louth (Lincolnshire)	14.30
March (Cambridgeshire)	14.30
Fowlmere, near Royston (Hertfordshire)	14.45
Stony Stratford, near Wolverton (Buckinghamshire)	14.45
Norwich (Norfolk)	15.00
Wymondham (Norfolk)	15.20
Clacton-on-Sea (Essex)	16.00

CHAPTER 6

Pollution

Air pollution

Why is air pollution a hazard?

After spending most of a day indoors, you may be told by your parents to go outside for 'a breath of fresh air'. But our air is far from fresh or healthy. Since the Industrial Revolution we have filled it with waste from burning fuels. This unwanted and harmful waste creates **air pollution**.

There are two types of waste, gases and solids, both of which cause a variety of harmful effects to us and to the land we live on.

Figure 6.1 shows the waste belched out from chimneys in Dusseldorf, Germany. The black smoke creates a dirty fog called **smog** which

Figure 6.2 The London smog

Figure 6.1 Air pollution from chimneys in Dusseldorf, Germany

reduces visibility, in the same way that fog does on motorways. As the smoke drifts in the wind it also damages buildings as the chemicals in it dissolve brick and metal. Inhaled by people, the dust in the smoke can damage lungs and lead to cancer. Further away from the industry, rain falling through the smoke becomes slightly acidic, so harming crops, forests and lakes. Air pollution, therefore, is damaging and can affect a very large area.

Perhaps one of the most serious incidents of air pollution was the London smog which lasted for days in December 1952 (see Figure 6.2). The black choking fog of dust and gas from domestic coal fires and local industries killed 4,000 sick and elderly people. Deaths resulted from bronchitis, influenza and pneumonia. Many thousand others suffered illnesses as a result of the same smog.

In Donora, Pennsylvania, USA, a smog caused 3 days of darkness, killed twenty people and caused 5,910 to fall ill, in October 1948.

These two dramatic events show that the main effect of air pollution on humans is to cause or worsen long-term illnesses. Breathing polluted air may not cause sudden death, as a volcanic eruption does, but it may shorten lives.

There has been a lot of publicity recently in Britain about the damage to children from lead emitted from car exhausts. Lead is a poison that can cause brain damage. In Manchester a study found that 4 per cent of children had lead blood levels higher than 0.8 parts per million, which is the level at which brain damage can occur.

Vegetation can be affected directly or indirectly by air pollution. Directly, dust and chemicals cause about $10 million worth of damage to vegetable crops annually in the USA. Trees and shrubs by the sides of motorways have been found to be stunted. A build-up of carbon dioxide in the atmosphere is thought to be forming a blanket, preventing heat escaping; this is called the **greenhouse effect**.

ACTIVITIES

1 Figure 6.3 shows Mexico City, probably the world's most polluted city, on a clear day and during a serious smog (look at the mountains). Describe some of the likely problems created by the smog. (Hints – health, light, heat of the sun, transport safety, and visibility.)

2 Figure 6.4 describes life in Mexico City.
  a List the effects of air pollution there.
  b What are the main causes of the air pollution?
  c How does the site of Mexico City make matters worse?

Figure 6.3a Mexico City on a clear day

b during a smog

In Mexico's capital you can catch hepatitis just by breathing, reports Christopher Reed
The city in a cloud of despair

At 7,400 feet high, Mexico City never had much oxygen to start off with.

The city lies sprawled across its plateau a mile and a half up, surrounded by still higher mountains. The bowl acts as a trap for smoke and fumes, and an estimated 11,000 tons of pollutants compete with the oxygen daily. On most days a brownish-grey smog haze hangs over the city, and the snow-capped twin peaks of the volcanos, Popocatepetl and Ixtaccihautl, only 40 miles away, are seen so rarely now that their visibility are occasions for comment in the newspapers.

The impact on the visitor accustomed to reasonable air is unpleasant and immediate. Within half an hour of arriving at the airport, I had a sore throat.

A city health officer has publicly reported that just breathing the air is equivalent to smoking 40 cigarettes a day.

The city is literally killing its inhabitants. Thousands die annually from diseases directly caused by or related to the contamination and pollution.

Pollutants come from the area's 130,000 industries, many belching uncontrolled smoke, and the 2.7 million vehicles that circulate – ricochet would be a better word – in the metropolis, causing a rush hour that lasts all day.

Medical researchers have stated that as many as half the city's residents, usually the poorest, die of parasitical diseases. About 40 per cent suffer from chronic bronchitis, and respiratory diseases are a major killer. Air pollution has been estimated at 100 times above the acceptable level.

The *Guardian*, 20 January 1984

Figure 6.4

How is air pollution caused?

The gases and solids which are emitted into the air are called **pollutants**. Figure 6.5 shows the main pollutants, their sources and some of their effects.

A study of pollution in the USA in 1972 showed that of the 140 million tonnes of air pollutants, 60 per cent came from vehicles, 14 per cent from power stations, 18 per cent from industry and 8 per cent from heating and refuse burning. Vehicles produce vast quantities of the gas carbon monoxide, along with lead and a range of minor gases. Power stations producing 'clean' electricity are in fact responsible for most of the sulphur dioxide emitted into the atmosphere. It is this that causes **acid rain**.

A whole range of industries produce

ACTIVITIES

3 a Study Figure 6.5. What are the two main sources of air pollution?

b Copy Figure 6.6 showing pollutants and their sources. Use Figure 6.5 to help you label gases and solids.

Figure 6.5 Some major air pollutants

Pollutant	Source	Effects
Gases		
carbon monoxide	vehicles	Human ill-health. Heart disease. Affects urban areas. Average concentration 10 ppm (parts per million). 10 ppm causes medical damage; 1,000 ppm kills. Often exceeds 100 ppm in Oxford Circus.
carbon dioxide	burning fossil fuels	Possibly leads to warming of atmosphere.
sulphur dioxide	burning fossil fuels chemical works	Makes rain water acidic, that is, **acid rain**. Kills plants and animals. Destroys lakes and forests. Also harmful to humans.
Solids/particles		
lead	vehicles	80 per cent of lead in petrol is emitted into atmosphere. Causes brain damage in children.
asbestos	sprayed on buildings to give support	50 per cent escapes into air. Fibres are very damaging to lungs and can lead to cancer there.
mercury	burning fossil fuels	Not known.
hydrochloric acid	burning plastic waste	Damage to lungs if inhaled.
pesticides	sprayed on agricultural land	50 per cent of the spray often remains in the air. Damage to wildlife and humans.
radioactive particles	nuclear power station	Possibly causes leukemia in children – controversial point.
fly ash	burning fossil fuels	Dust and ash can cause smogs and damage vegetation.

Figure 6.6 Air pollutants and their sources

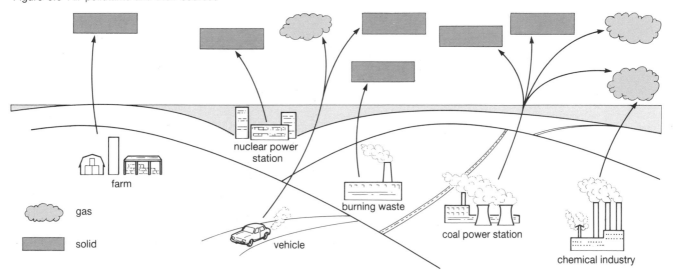

pollutants. A factory handling asbestos caused many deaths from asbestosis (lung disease) at Hebdon Bridge, Yorkshire. Brickworks in Bedfordshire were found to produce fluorine, which damaged nearby pastures and caused cattle disease.

To summarise, there are a number of damaging pollutants, both gases and solids, which can harm humans, farmland and buildings. There are also several pollution sources, vehicles and power stations being the chief culprits.

Can air pollution be prevented?

There are a number of ways of preventing air pollution.

1 Government laws

In Britain, following the London smog of 1952, the Government passed the Clean Air Act in 1956. This prevents industries belching out black smoke. It also identifies **smoke control areas** in towns and cities; only smokeless fuels may be used there. We in Britain no longer suffer from severe smogs.

2 Filter systems

There are many filter systems which can be installed in tall chimney stacks to remove pollutants. One such device is the **electrostatic precipitator** (see Figure 6.7). Solid particles passing into the precipitator are given a negative electrical charge. They are attracted to the positively charged sides, to fall to the bottom of the device as dust. The dust can be collected and removed. Removing gases is more expensive and devices are not used widely.

3 Vehicles

Vehicle pollution can be reduced by altering exhaust systems and by keeping vehicles out of town centres by creating pedestrian precincts. Lead pollution can be restricted by the use of lead-free petrol. West Germany is to introduce this in 1986 and other European countries are likely to follow suit in 1989.

ACTIVITIES

4 Figure 6.8 shows the changes in smoke emission from burning coal in the United Kingdom.
   a Produce a bar graph to show these changes. Use the *total* figures to draw each bar and, using a colour key, sub-divide the bar into the main sources.
   b Does air pollution appear to have been reduced in the United Kingdom?
   c Can you explain the fact that railways stopped producing smoke from 1970 onwards?
   d Give some reasons for the drop in: domestic smoke emission, industrial smoke emission.

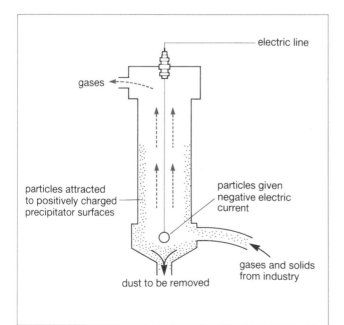

Figure 6.7 Electrostatic precipitator

Year	Sources			Total
	Domestic	Industry	Railways	
1958	1.28	0.51	0.22	2.01
1960	1.21	0.35	0.19	1.75
1965	0.95	0.14	0.06	1.15
1970	0.64	0.08	—	0.72
1971	0.55	0.06	—	0.61
1972	0.45	0.05	—	0.50
1973	0.44	0.05	—	0.49
1974	0.42	0.04	—	0.40
1975	0.35	0.04	—	0.39
1976	0.33	0.04	—	0.37
1977	0.34	0.04	—	0.38
1978	0.30	0.03	—	0.33
1979	0.31	0.04	—	0.35
1980	0.25	0.03	—	0.28
1981	0.24	0.03	—	0.27
1982	0.24	0.03	—	0.27

Figure 6.8 Changes in smoke emission from burning coal in the UK

Acid rain

Why is acid rain a hazard?

During the early 1980s there has been a lot of publicity about so-called **acid rain** and the harm that it is doing to forests, lakes and buildings. A survey carried out in 1983 showed that 34 per cent of forest in West Germany is damaged, while 20,000 lakes in Norway and Sweden are acidic enough to damage fish and 4,000 are completely lifeless. Also in Sweden acidic water is corroding copper pipes, causing diarrhoea in children and even turning hair green after washing! The Acropolis in Athens, Greece, has deteriorated as much in the last 20 years as in the previous 2,000 years. The blame for all this has been put on acid rain.

How is acid rain caused?

The rain that falls to earth is not pure water. As it falls through the atmosphere is picks up carbon dioxide and becomes weak **carbonic acid** which is relatively harmless. However, if the atmosphere is full of pollutants, especially sulphur dioxide and nitrogen oxide, the rainwater becomes more acidic. It becomes weak nitric or sulphuric acid. It is these stronger acids which damage plants, fish and buildings.

Figure 6.9 explains acidity and the effects it has on life.

ACTIVITIES

5 a The information displayed in Figure 6.10 can be shown as a bar chart. For each country draw two bars, side by side, one showing total emission and the other total deposition. Use a different colour for emission and deposition. To help you the figures for Denmark and France have been plotted on Figure 6.11. Copy this diagram and complete the graph.

  b In which countries is sulphur emission greater than deposition?
    In which countries is sulphur emission less than deposition?
    Study Figure 6.12, which shows the prevailing winds in Europe. Can the prevailing winds help to explain your answers to the first two questions?
    Do you thing it is fair that many European countries blame Britain for causing acid rain?

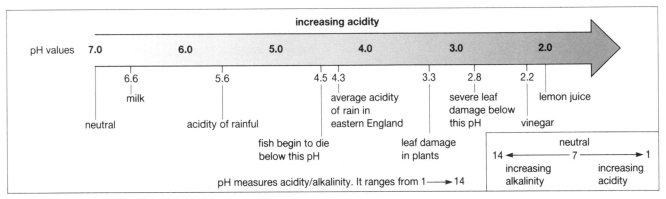

Figure 6.9 Acidity and its effects on life

Country	Million tonnes sulphur per year	
	Total emission	Total deposition
Denmark	0.20	0.10
France	1.55	1.30
Norway	0.05	0.30
Netherlands	0.25	0.20
Poland	1.25	1.40
Britain	2.10	1.00
Sweden	0.25	0.60
West Germany	1.70	1.25
East Germany	2.05	0.90

Figure 6.10 Sulphur emissions and depositions in Europe

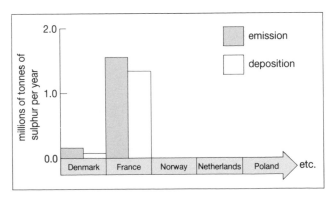

Figure 6.11

What are the solutions to acid rain?

In 1983 40 million tonnes of sulphur dioxide were poured into the skies above Europe. Britain produced more than any other European country. Over 50 per cent of this was emitted from power stations. The obvious solution is to reduce the amount of pollution. Figure 6.13 describes possible technical solutions. As you can see, the main problem is expense. Electricity prices could rise by 20 per cent!

The European Economic Community is keen to reduce sulphur dioxide emissions dramatically, although Britain wants more research to determine absolutely what it is that causes the widespread damage; there may be causes other than acid rain.

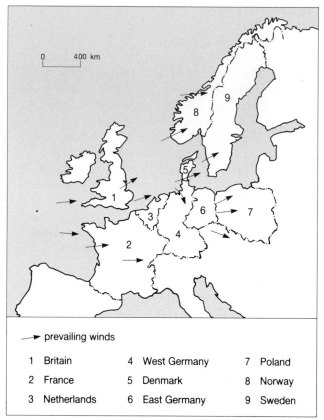

Figure 6.12 Prevailing winds in north-west Europe

→ prevailing winds

1	Britain	4	West Germany	7	Poland
2	France	5	Denmark	8	Norway
3	Netherlands	6	East Germany	9	Sweden

ACTIVITIES

6   Governments trying to solve the acid rain problem have to make a difficult decision. If they decide to reduce emissions, the price of electricity will rise, but if they do nothing, then damage to environments will continue. What would you decide to do? Give reasons for your answer.

Solution	Details	Any problems
low sulphur fuels	Use low sulphur coal stocks; North Sea oil is also a reliable low sulphur energy source.	Oil is not common and is expensive to extract. Coal-fired power stations need to be fitted with pollution control equipment.
desulphurisation	Filter system in chimney flues to trap sulphur.	Expensive. Creates an unpleasant waste.
fluidised bed combustion	New low temperature boiler which uses limestone to absorb sulphur dioxide.	Expensive.
liming	Addition of lime to lakes to reduce acidity.	Messy. Only temporary effect. Expensive.
cleaning up	Replantation of trees; addition of alkalines to soil; scrubbing clean buildings; etc.	Only temporary effect. Very expensive.

Figure 6.13 Possible solutions to acid rain

Water pollution

Why is water pollution a hazard?

Water can be called **polluted** when it is not suitable for its intended use, for example, drinking, irrigation, recreation.

Polluted water can cause illness in humans and animals, can destroy water wildlife and can be unpleasant for recreation.

In the Third World the vast majority of people do not have safe drinking water, as we in Britain do. In rural areas only 29 per cent of the peasants have safe water while the rest obtain their drinking water from polluted streams and wells. The polluted water becomes a breeding ground for diseases such as typhoid, cholera and dysentery, which kill many thousands every year. Even in Britain polluted water caused a typhoid epidemic, in Croydon in 1938!

Water wildlife suffers from pollution. Chemicals

Figure 6.14 The effects of water pollution

ACTIVITIES

7 a Describe the effects of water pollution.

b What do you think are the causes of water pollution?

8 Copy Figure 6.15, which shows the main sources of water pollution in rivers. Add the following labels in the appropriate places (1–5):

A chemicals and hot water
B livestock wastes
C hot water and possible nuclear wastes
D domestic sewage and household waste
E chemicals from pesticides and fertilisers.

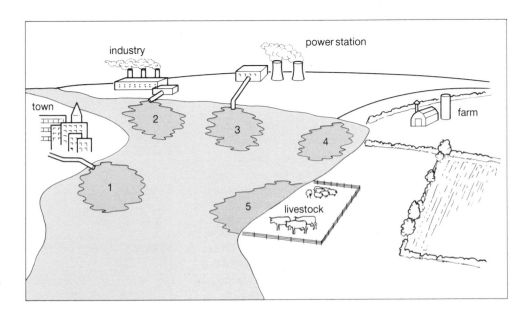

Figure 6.15 Main sources of water pollution

in the water use up the oxygen, so causing fish to suffocate and die. Figure 6.14 shows dead fish, the result of water pollution. Since fish is an important source of food in many parts of the world, water pollution is a great problem.

Dead fish, foam and unpleasant smells greatly affect the appeal of water recreation and leisure. No-one wants to fish, swim or even walk alongside badly polluted water. Tourism in Spain and southern France is beginning to be affected as pollution in the Mediterranean Sea causes holidaymakers to suffer from upset stomachs after swimming or from food poisoning after eating shellfish.

How is water pollution caused?

Water can easily become a dumping ground for man since it appears to remove what is dumped in it. There are many causes of water pollution, as shown in Figure 6.15.

Sewage is the main pollutant of water. It used to be discharged raw throughout the world but nowadays countries in the Developed World have sewers to deal with it. In the Third World, however, the situation is very different. Rivers and water holes serve as combined toilets, baths and washhouses. (see Figure 6.16) Human and animal waste is washed into rivers where it infects the water so that drinking or just standing in the water can cause disease. The following account describes conditions in a poor part of Bogota, Colombia:

'There is no piped water supply for the settlement. Water comes from a stream more than a mile away. In the evenings children go down with battered old pans and oil cans, fill them and stagger home with them strung from bamboo poles. The stream is grossly polluted, mostly by the excretia of residents. No sewers have been provided. Only a minority of residents have

Figure 6.16

latrines and these are no more than pits dug in the earth. I asked the Penas (a family) if they had a latrine. They did not even know what the word meant. When I clarified Amparo replied 'Oh no, we're only poor peasants. We just go up the road in the bushes.'

Industrial waste is varied. A power station uses water for cooling. When this is returned to rivers it is up to 10°C warmer. This has quite a harmful effect on water life. Nuclear power stations may discharge radioactive waste which can be very dangerous. In 1984 radioactive waste from Sellafield, Cumbria, was washed ashore where it polluted beaches. Following a considerable public outcry the beaches were closed for several weeks before being declared safe.

Paper, textile and chemical industries are the worst offenders, pumping a range of toxic chemicals into rivers. Sometimes waste is dumped at sea where it is claimed to be harmless. This is not always true, for in 1969 100,000 sea birds died in the Irish Sea, probably as a result of industrial dumping.

Agriculture is a recent polluter. Nowadays chemicals are used as pesticides or fertilisers and over the years these are washed into rivers. Nitrates turn into nitrites, harmful to both humans and animals. Livestock waste is washed into rivers also, adding to the pollution risk.

How can water pollution be prevented?

Water pollution in the Third World will probably last for many years. Indeed it may worsen. The solutions are simple but they take time and are expensive.

Fresh piped water would solve many problems. Where this has been introduced diseases have been reduced dramatically. For example, in East Africa cholera has been reduced by 90 per cent and typhoid by 80 per cent.

Improved sanitation would also help a great deal. An interesting solution involves collecting sewage in chambers to ferment, so turning it into fertiliser, which can be used safely on the land. The Oxfam sanitation unit does this. Over 50 have been installed in Bangladesh and many more are planned. The unit is very simple and takes only 4 men one day to erect. Figure 6.17 shows one being constructed. The squatting plates are connected underground by a central pipe. Flushing takes the sewage to tanks where fermentation kills germs such as cholera and typhoid. After about a week the sludge is put on the land as manure. In this simple, cheap and useful way, pollution and disease are reduced.

Figure 6.17 Oxfam sanitation unit being constructed

In Britain we are much more able to cope with water pollution. The ten regional water authorities, set up in 1974, impose strict regulations on industrial pollutants. Rivers are surveyed regularly to check pollution levels. Consequently nearly 80 per cent of all rivers and canals are free from dangerous pollution and only about 1 per cent are grossly polluted.

Domestic and industrial waste is processed by many hundred sewage works, located throughout the country. Figure 6.18 describes the operation of a typical sewage works. Notice than the main aim is to separate solid waste and sludge from liquid. The liquid is purified gradually, before being discharged into rivers. The sludge undergoes a lengthy cleaning process before being taken away, either to be used on the land or dumped at sea.

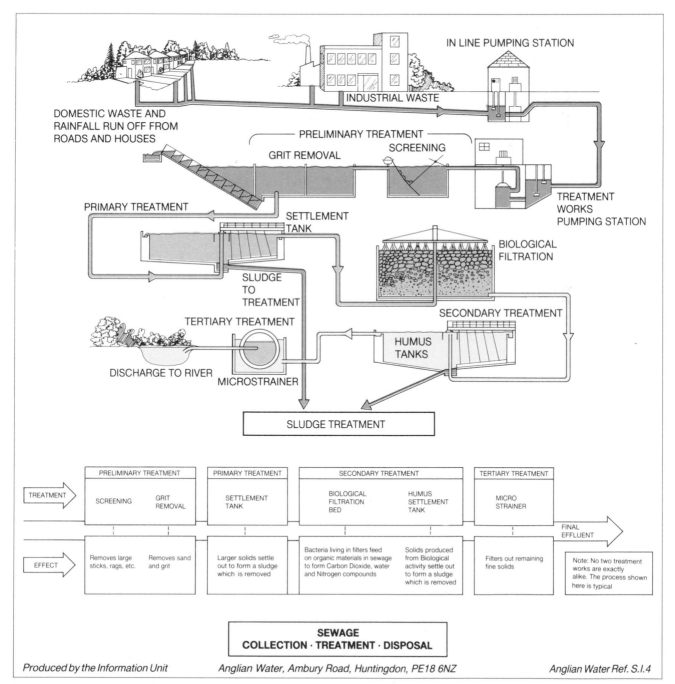

Figure 6.18 The operation of a sewage works

Figure 6.19 Broadholme sewage works

a

b

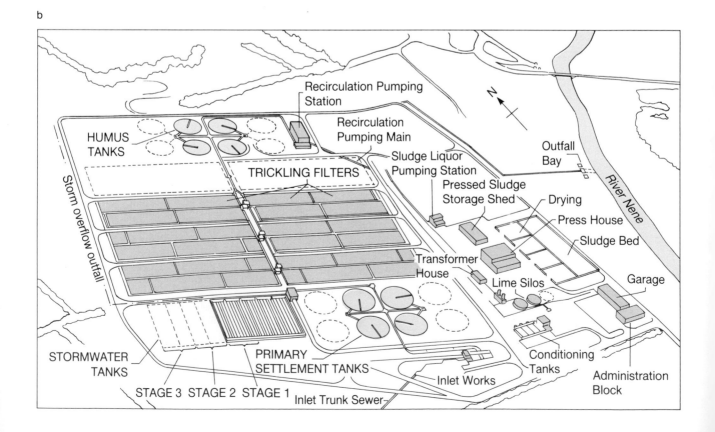

9 a Figure 6.19(a) is a photograph and (b) a plan of the Broadholme Sewage Works near Wellingborough, Northamptonshire. Make a labelled sketch of the photograph and use the plan to identify and label the following:

   1 River Nene
   2 access road running around the edge of the works
   3 primary settlement tanks
   4 filtration tanks
   5 humus tanks
   6 inlet works and preliminary treatment
   7 route of inlet trunk sewer
   8 outfall pipe into River Nene
   9 sludge processing works
   10 north point

   b Draw a series of arrows to show the movement of sewage from one stage to the next.
   c The sewage works is in the middle of the countryside. Why do you think this is?
   d As the sewers also collect rainfall, it is possible for them to be overloaded following a period of heavy rain. Is there anything at the works to cope with this?

10 Figure 6.20 shows two methods of sewage disposal into the sea, as used by the Welsh Water Authority. Diagram A is the old-fashioned method which is being replaced by the modern method in diagram B.
   a What effect would short sea outfall have on: a local fishing industry that catches shellfish in the estuary?
   the popularity of Seaford's local beach?
   b Would you expect sewage to be carried inland to West Seaford and beyond if the short sea outfall method was being used. Explain your answer.
   c Describe and explain the advantages of the long sea outfall.
   d Can you think of any problems that might arise with long sea outfall?

Figure 6.20 Sewage disposal methods

a Short sea outfall

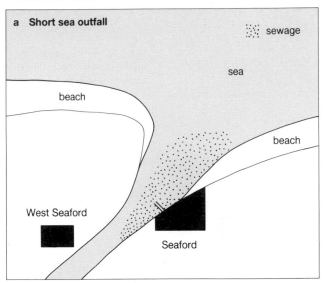

b Long sea outfall

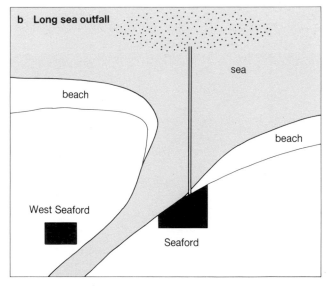

Oil pollution

In March 1967 an oil supertanker ran aground off Cornwall and 110,000 tonnes of crude oil formed a vast slick which soon spread to nearby beaches. Over 5,600 sea birds were killed, 100 kilometres of coastline contaminated and untold damage done to the marine life. Such dramatic incidents account for only 4 per cent of all oil pollution at sea. Figure 6.21 shows the different sources of oil pollution.

Oil pollution has only recently become a serious problem, since oil companies have developed huge tankers to carry crude oil across the oceans (see Figure 6.22). The largest tankers are now well over 500,000 tonnes. Such tankers are not easily controlled; a 250,000 tonne tanker takes about half an hour to stop!

Oil slicks are difficult to treat. Ideally some sort of bacteria which would break down the oil, like those that break down sewage, could be used, but, unfortunately, one has not yet been discovered. In Britain, detergent is used to clear beaches, but this is often more harmful to wildlife than the oil itself. There is no obvious solution to the oil hazard.

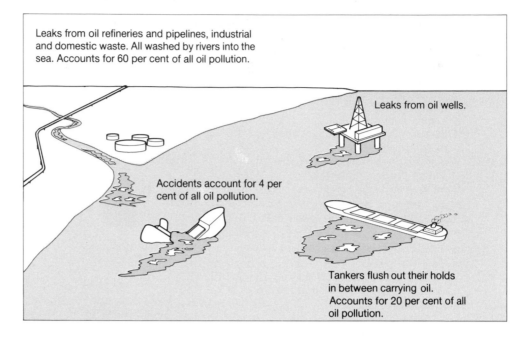

Figure 6.21 Sources of marine oil pollution

Figure 6.22 The 250,000 tonne *Esso Demetia* berthed at Milford Haven

ACTIVITIES

11 Figure 6.23 shows the incidents of coastal pollution in Britain in 1977. The coastline has been divided into sections, each one numbered. The number indicates the number of incidents for that section of coast.

a Using either tracing paper or an outline map, colour the coastline to show the severity of pollution. Use the following colour key:

pollution	number of incidents	colour
No pollution	0	Pencil or thin black line
Slight pollution	1–4	Yellow
Moderate pollution	5–10	Orange
Severe pollution	11+	Red

You will end with a multi-coloured coastline!

b Next to those sections of coast with severe pollution (red), write the number of incidents.

c Using Figure 6.23 mark the following on your map:
oil refineries;
direction of prevailing wind;
the English Channel;
the North Sea.

d Which stretch of coastline is most severely polluted?

e Where is the longest stretch of unpolluted coastline?

f Is there any relationship between oil refineries and pollution? Why do you think this is?

g There are no refineries and few large towns along the stretch of coast in south Cornwall marked (X). How can the severe pollution here be explained?

h As North Sea oil production increases, which parts of the British coast would you expect to suffer increased pollution from oil?

i Most oil tanker collisions around Britain occur in the English Channel. Why do you think this is?

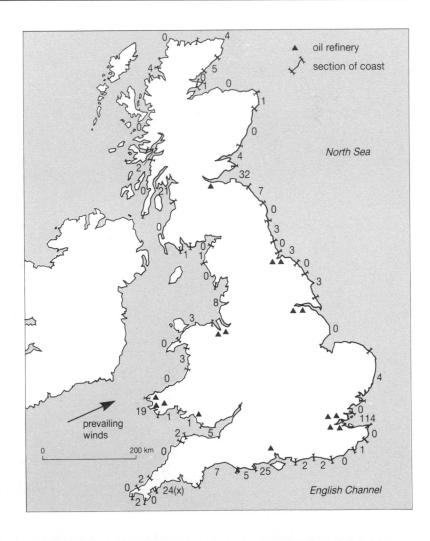

Figure 6.23 Oil pollution incidents affecting the British coastline, 1977

Land pollution

You have only to walk alongside a road or river to notice that the British are a 'throw-away' society. Town centres are littered with cardboard boxes, sweet wrappers and fish and chip papers. Apart from being unpleasant to look at, litter and waste can harm soil, pollute water and form breeding grounds for pests. Figure 6.24 shows a typical collection of waste.

Piles of old motor cars are a common sight now by the sides of railways or in industrial areas. When a car fails its MOT or is labelled a 'write off' after an accident, it is scrapped, perhaps sold for as little as £5 to a breaker's yard. In Britain in 1967 325,000 cars were discarded, 600,000 in 1970 and 1,300,000 in 1980. Over 12,000,000 tyres are discarded every year, usually to be burnt.

In 1979 in Britain we threw away 6,000 million glass containers and 9,000 million cans, enough to build seven columns to the moon!

Industry also produces a great deal of solid waste. Whilst the bulk of it is harmless, such as ash, dirt and metal, about 11,000,000 tonnes of toxic waste is produced annually. There is also nuclear waste to be disposed of.

ACTIVITIES

12 Study Figure 6.24.
   a Identify the different types of domestic waste.
   b What seems to be the most common type?

13 List some of the types of waste that you would expect from the following sources: households, gardens, building demolition, towns and cities, industry.

Figure 6.24

14 Figure 6.25 shows the changing composition of domestic waste in Britain.

a Work out the total waste for each year.

b Has there been an increase or decrease between 1940 and 1980? Why do you think this is?

c Draw a line graph to show the information. Represent each type of waste with a different coloured line. Label the vertical axis 'Average weight per person per day (grams)' and the horizontal axis 'Date'.

d Describe and try to explain the changing trends for each type of waste.

e What changes do you think will occur between 1980 and 2000?

f Suggest some methods of disposal for the different types of domestic waste.

	Average weight per person per day (grams)				
	1940	1950	1960	1970	1980
dust and cinders	362	317	272	158	113
paper	91	113	136	226	294
plastics	0	0	0	23	45
rotting vegetation	91	91	91	113	136
metals	23	45	45	68	68
glass	23	45	45	45	91
rags	23	23	23	23	23
others	45	45	45	23	23
total					

Figure 6.25 Changing composition of domestic waste in Britain, 1940–80

Figure 6.26 An open dump

How can waste be disposed?

The vast majority of waste is disposed of by dumping, much of which is controlled. On land mines and quarries are filled in with waste, at sea waste decomposes in the ocean depths.

There are a number of possibilities for waste disposal.

1 Open dumps

Figure 6.26 shows a typical open dump. This is the most common form of disposal. It usually involves the filling of ground depressions and hollows.

2 Sanitary landfill

This is a more controlled type of disposal. Alternate layers of waste and soil are used to fill depressions or quarries. Each layer is levelled mechanically before the next layer is added.

3 Incineration

Up to 95 per cent of the volume of waste can be burned and this method of disposal is becoming more common, especially as it can generate electricity.

4 Swine feed

In many parts of the world waste can be fed to animals which are not particular about their food, goats, for example. In USA about one-quarter of all waste is given to pigs.

5 Composting

Certain types of soft, rotting garbage can be used as fertiliser.

6 Recycling

Pressure groups like the Friends of the Earth have recently campaigned to encourage industry to recycle products. As a result many towns in Britain now have bottle banks where glass items can be dumped for later recycling (see Figure 6.27). In Germany a large amount of toilet paper and writing paper is produced from recycled paper. In the future it seems likely that tin cans will be recycled for their aluminium content. Each can costs about 10 pence to make so the saving would be great if they were recycled, like milk bottles at present. The Friends of the Earth estimate that recycling cans and bottles would save 600,000 tonnes of raw materials and £100 million for the consumer each year.

Old cars are broken up for spares and scrap metal now forms a vital raw material for many of the world's steelworks.

Figure 6.27

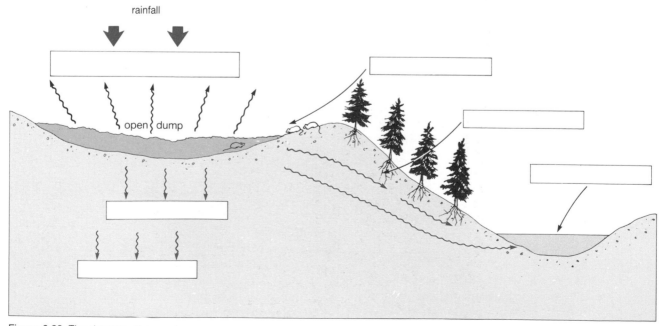

Figure 6.28 The dangers of open dumps

Figure 6.29 The method of waste disposal

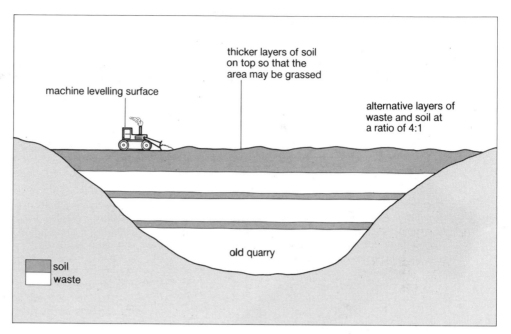

machine levelling surface

thicker layers of soil on top so that the area may be grassed

alternative layers of waste and soil at a ratio of 4:1

old quarry

soil
waste

Figure 6.30 A Friends of the Earth poster

ACTIVITIES

15 Carry out a study of the disposal of waste in your local area.
  a Look at roadsides, country lanes, woods and recreation grounds, canals and rivers to discover what sort of things people dump carelessly.
  b How do you think such dumping could be stopped?
  c Contact your local council department to find out the methods of waste disposal in your area.

16 a Figure 6.28 shows the dangers of open dumps. Copy it and add the following labels in the correct boxes:
    damage to roots of vegetation
    contamination of groundwater
    contamination of rivers
    breeding ground for pests
    contamination of soil
    bad smells
  b How could these dangers be prevented?

17 Figure 6.29 shows a method of waste disposal.
  a What is the method of disposal shown in the diagram?
  b Describe what is happening.
  c Once complete, what sort of things could the site be used for?
  d What is the long-term problem associated with this type of disposal? (Think about what is needed for this method and what could run out).

18 Figure 6.30 is a poster encouraging recycling tin cans. Design a poster yourself to encourage either the recycling of bottles or tin cans.

ACTIVITIES

19 Nuclear waste at Billingham: a public enquiry.
Proposal It is proposed that waste from nuclear power stations be dumped in old mine workings 130 metres below the surface of Billingham, Humberside. Waste will be stored in concrete drums in the underground tunnels and when full, the whole mine will be sealed with concrete. Figure 6.31 shows the location of the mine.

a Public enquiry details. Divide the class to provide the following characters:
  1 overall Chairperson, to keep order, to call speakers, etc.
  2 leader of campaign **for** proposal, and
  3 leader of campaign **against** proposal (co-ordinates case, introduces case, calls his/her speakers, concludes case, etc.)
  4 expert speakers to put forward different points of view. See Figure 6.32.
  5 jury (rest of class), to decide what to do.

b Preparation. A successful enquiry depends on thorough preparation.
  The leaders must decide their introductory and concluding speeches and the order in which their experts are to be called.
  The experts must prepare their speeches (2–3 minutes each), using Figure 6.32 as a guide, added to by extra research.
  The jury must think of questions to ask both sides as it is important that they make the right decision.
  A map of the proposed scheme would be useful for reference.

c The enquiry:
Chairperson reads the proposal;
Chairperson calls the leader of the campaign **for** to deliver his/her case. Leader introduces the case, calls each expert in turn and then sums up. The case **against** is presented. Chairperson takes questions from the jury. The leaders either answer themselves or pass the question to one of their experts. This part of the enquiry usually decides the outcome as each side can be put under pressure by the jury. The jury votes on the proposal, taking into account the strengths and weaknesses of the arguments put forward by each side.

Figure 6.31

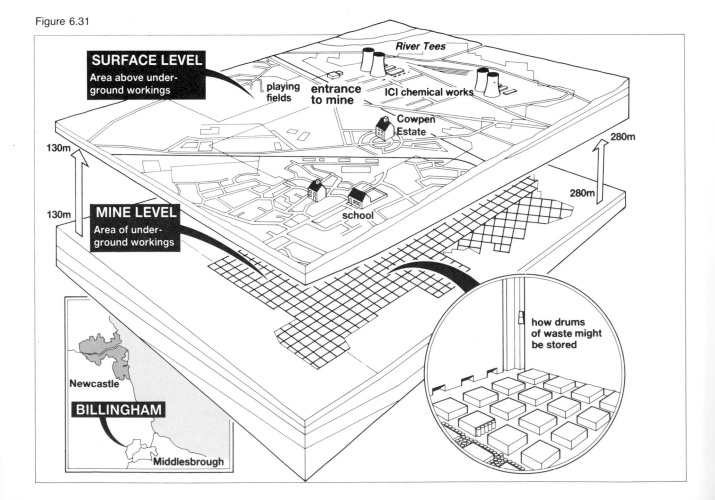

SURFACE LEVEL
Area above underground workings

River Tees

playing fields
entrance to mine
ICI chemical works
Cowpen Estate
130m
280m
280m

MINE LEVEL
Area of underground workings

130m

school

how drums of waste might be stored

Newcastle

BILLINGHAM

Middlesbrough

THE CASE FOR

Person	Point of view
Mr McFlue British Nuclear Fuels	At present over 35,000 cubic metres of nuclear waste are waiting to be disposed. A site must be found soon if nuclear power stations are to continue.
Sir Reginald Bifton Government Energy Secretary	Nuclear power is the energy of the future. With coal and oil running out we must expand our nuclear power programme, but this can only be done if a site for waste is found. Billingham is ideal. It must be used or our nation will suffer!
Mr Bullock Nuclear industry radioactive waste executive	People are stupid! They do not seem to understand that all the waste needs is to be left alone. In a sealed container it is perfectly harmless!

THE CASE AGAINST

Person	Point of view
Mr and Mrs Green Live on Cowpen Estate	We are worried about the proposal. Nobody knows what the waste will do when it is underground. It is like a time bomb. Who wants to live on top of a nuclear time bomb?
Mr Pringle Local councillor	Why Billingham? This is an area of high unemployment. We are trying to attract new industry. What sensible businessman would build a factory over a nuclear dump?
Miss Jenkin Friends of the Earth	The nuclear industry must prove without doubt that this is scientifically the best site in Britain. Is it being chosen for political reasons? Why not use the salt mines in Tory Cheshire? The possible damage to the environment is unthinkable.
Mr Pike Hydrologist	There is a possibility that water might seep into the nuclear dump and then contaminate groundwater. This could be extremely dangerous to the public and might do untold damage to soil which might affect crops in turn.
Dr Boyle Medical adviser	Nuclear waste is dangerous. Plutonium can cause cancer if it gets into the blood stream or the lungs. These wastes require a special kind of storage so that man would not come into contact with them for tens of thousands of years.
Mrs Witt Resident of Billingham	The mine workings are so close. When they were being worked there was a noise like a concrete roller being dragged along under the house. I am terrified at the thought of nuclear waste under my house. Being a pensioner I cannot move away.

Figure 6.32

CHAPTER 7

Surface instability

What is surface instability?

The surface of the land may appear to be completely safe but there are many areas where movement has occurred or may occur. This movement can be downhill in the form of a **landslide** or an **avalanche** or can be **vertical subsidence**, collapse into an old mine shaft, for example. The main hazard of surface instability is that it usually happens suddenly without any warning signs. This chapter studies landslides, avalanches and subsidence.

Landslides

What is the landslide hazard?

A landslide is the downhill movement of material. It is a common and usually harmless event. However, there have been notable landslides which have caused loss of life and a great deal of damage. Figure 7.1 (a–c) gives a few examples of the landslide hazard.

Figure 7.1 Some major landslides

a Vaiont, Italy

On 9 October 1963 a combination of 2 months of heavy rainfall and many small earthquakes caused a massive landslide to occur on the steep southern side of the Vaiont Reservoir. About 240,000,000 cubic metres of rock slid into the reservoir in less than 30 seconds. It filled in about a third of the reservoir, creating huge waves, the largest of which topped the dam by some 100 metres before crashing into the valley below. Over 2,600 people were killed.

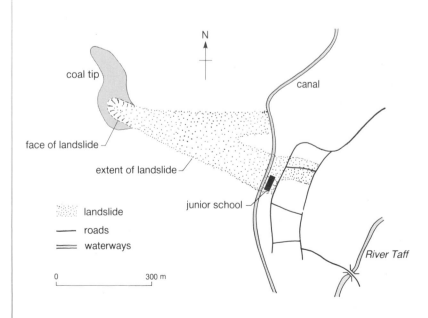

coal tip

N

canal

face of landslide

extent of landslide

junior school

River Taff

landslide

roads

waterways

0   300 m

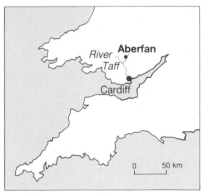

River
Taff

Aberfan

Cardiff

0   50 km

b Aberfan, Wales

On 21 October 1966 a huge coal tip collapsed following heavy rainfall, sending a black river of sludge into the village of Aberfan. A total of 147 people were killed, of whom 116 were schoolchildren gathered in the local school for morning assembly. After the landslide it was discovered that the coal waste had been dumped on top of a spring.

c Anchorage, Alaska

Anchorage is built on fairly soft clayey rock and during the 1964 earthquake (see Chapter 1) hundreds of landslides occurred. The landscape suddenly became a jumbled mass of earth and buildings as houses were wrecked and service pipes ruptured. In all 300 million dollars worth of damage was caused.

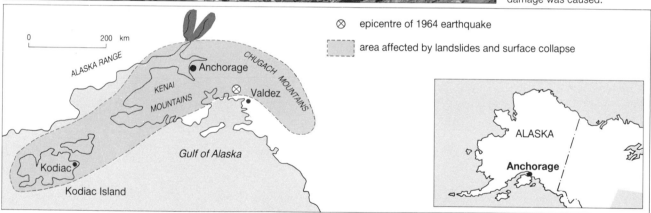

⊗ epicentre of 1964 earthquake

▨ area affected by landslides and surface collapse

ACTIVITIES

1 a Study Figure 7.1. Do the landslides appear to have been sudden or gradual events?

  b Since the beginning of the century over 200,000 people have been killed by landslides. Use your answer to 1a to suggest reasons for this high death toll.

2 Imagine that you are a news reporter in Anchorage and that you are filming the scene as shown by Figure 7.1(c). Describe the scene to your viewers. Tell them about the effects of the landslide.

3 Refer back to the descriptions of the landslides and answer the following:

  a What two major factors do you think 'triggered off' the landslides?

  b Try to explain why these two factors should have this effect.

  c Try to identify some other factors from the descriptions that may have encouraged the landslides to occur. For each factor say why you think it may encourage landslides.

How are landslides caused?

As a landslide involves the movement of material (soil, debris, rock) downhill, a slope is essential. Most of the time material on a slope will remain **stable**; if the slope becomes **unstable** a landslide results.

There are many factors which may make a slope unstable. The steepness of the slope may be increased as debris is dumped on it or part of it is excavated. If houses are built they will exert a downward pressure and if vegetation is removed the binding of the soil by roots will no longer occur. Weak or saturated material such as clay or the coal waste at Aberfan will move easily.

Although there are many factors which encourage landslides it is usually the 'triggering off' factors (see Activity 3a) that actually start a landslide. Figure 7.2 shows a hillside that is very likely to have a landslide.

ACTIVITIES

4 Study Figure 7.3
  a Is this slope stable or unstable? Explain your answer.
  b Would you buy house X? Explain your answer.
  c A plan to build a power station (Y) has been rejected on the grounds that it may cause a landslide. Do you agree with this decision?
  d Discuss some possible measures that would make landslides less likely on this slope.

Figure 7.2 A hillslope likely to have a landslide

HEAVY RAINFALL
this will saturate the soil and encourage movement

BUILDINGS
increases weight on slope and adds to downward pull of gravity

STEEP SLOPE

ROCK TYPE
weak saturated material or shattered rock is more likely to move than solid bedrock

REMOVAL OF VEGETATION
roots bind the soil together. Vegetation uses up some of the soil moisture

BEDROCK
solid bedrock below weak material: the junction forms the likely *slide plane*

PERMEABILITY
water flowing on surface of impermeable layer

EXCAVATION
undercutting of slope increases instability

bedding plane

Figure 7.3 A coastal hillslope

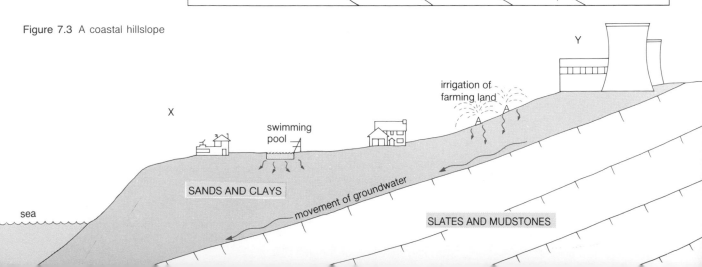

Y

irrigation of farming land

X

swimming pool

SANDS AND CLAYS

movement of groundwater

SLATES AND MUDSTONES

sea

Can landslides be prevented?

There are a number of ways in which potentially hazardous slopes can be stabilised. The type of method used depends on the costs and benefits, that is, how much damage might be caused by a landslide. Some methods are listed below:

1 Surface drainage: diversion of surface streams from the slope.
2 Groundwater drainage: pipes will drain soil and prevent saturation.
3 Artificial structures: building of terraces or walls to prevent major slides; bolting of rock to stop rockfalls, for example, the Avon gorge at Bristol.
4 Planting vegetation; binds soils together.

For planning, a **landslide hazard map** is useful as it outlines a danger zone. Such a hazard map is drawn up by examining historical records of landslides and looking for the sorts of factors likely to encourage landslides.

Avalanches

What is the avalanche hazard?

An avalanche is a mass of snow or ice that moves very rapidly down a mountainside. Many thousands occur every year in the mountain areas of the world with only a few causing any real damage. In Switzerland an average of twenty-five people are killed every year by avalanches.

Avalanches are very sudden events which only last a matter of minutes. They are, however, extremely powerful and move very rapidly, sometimes at speeds exceeding 300 kph. They will flatten trees and carve a path through villages, so causing a great deal of destruction. Figure 7.4 shows an avalanche.

Figure 7.4 An avalanche!

The destruction caused by an avalanche is due to the combination of the weight of snow and ice and the gusts of air formed as the avalanche speeds downhill. Figure 7.6 explains the force of an avalanche.

ACTIVITIES

5 Norway suffers about the same number of avalanches as Switzerland but only twelve people die on average a year. Why do you think Switzerland has more deaths?

6 Read the newspaper articles in Figure 7.5
  a Which people appear at most risk from avalanches?
  b Generally more tourists are killed than local people. Why do you think this is so?

7 a What are the three forces that together form the impact of an avalanche?
  b Which is the most destructive?

8 Does the avalanche in Figure 7.6 contain much snow? Explain your answer.

9 How important do you think the steepness of the slope is in determining the impact of an avalanche? Explain your answer.

Swiss avalanche sweeps teachers to their deaths

Two British women teachers were swept to their deaths yesterday in an avalanche in Switzerland. Several children in their charge were buried under snow, but were uninjured. Two ski instructors were also believed killed.

The dead teachers were Mrs Lynn Bonnet, who was in charge of 21 children from Edgehill College, Bideford north Devon, and Miss Karen Money, who was with 28 pupils from St Felix School, Southwold, Suffolk. Both were in their twenties.

The avalanche happened in the village of Saas Grund, near Saas Fee, where nearly 100 British children and staff from three schools were holidaying.

The holidays were organised by Schools Abroad, of Haywards Heath, Sussex, and one of the children caught by the avalanche was Jonathan Hopkins, aged 16, whose father is managing director of the firm.

Mr Peter Hopkins said 'As I understand it, a big avalanche caught up a lot of skiers, including Jonathan, who managed to dig himself out and ski back to the village with an instructor to raise the alarm.

'The two teachers were killed, as were two ski instructors, but all the other children have been accounted for, and were not injured.

'Jonathan told me he had been ski-ing with the two teachers, the previous day, and I understand they were both competent skiers'.

Mr Hopkins was flying out last night to bring home the St Felix and Edgehill pupils.

The Guardian, 2 April 1984

Avalanches kill 13 on ski slopes

Rome (AFP and AP) – Avalanches killed 13 skiers over the weekend in France, Austria, Italy and Andorra, and six others were still missing this afternoon, authorities said.

In northern Italy four skiers were killed yesterday and five more were missing on slopes near Belluno.

Helicopters and boats rescued 200 people trapped by floods west of Rome as incessant rain, snow and high winds battered almost the whole of Italy, knocking out power and telephone lines and blocking roads.

The Times, 27 February 1984

Figure 7.5 Recent avalanches

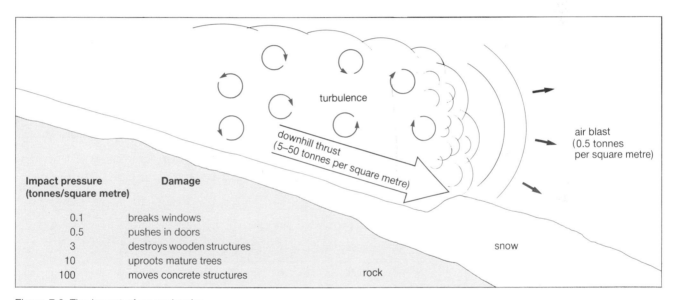

Impact pressure (tonnes/square metre)	Damage
0.1	breaks windows
0.5	pushes in doors
3	destroys wooden structures
10	uproots mature trees
100	moves concrete structures

Figure 7.6 The impact of an avalanche

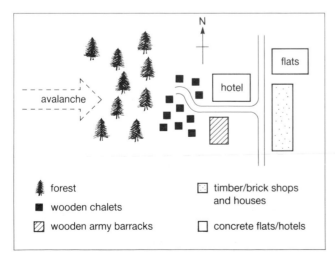

Figure 7.7 The village of Koldupir

How are avalanches caused?

When snow first settles on a slope it tends to stick to it. As more snow falls the weight of the packed snow gradually increases. Eventually the time may come when the weight of the snow along with the constant downward pull of gravity

ACTIVITIES

10 A major avalanche is moving rapidly towards the fictional village of Koldupir, as shown in Figure 7.7. By referring to Figure 7.7 give a detailed description of the likely effects of the avalanche as it passes into the village. Assume that it is as powerful as the one shown in Figure 7.6.

causes a portion of snow to break away and slide downhill, forming an avalanche.

The start of an avalanche is very sudden and may occur as the result of an earthquake or an explosion. Even skiing may trigger off an avalanche!

Figure 7.8 shows the two main types of avalanche. Some start from a single point and get gradually larger as they move downhill (the snowball effect!) Others occur when a slab of

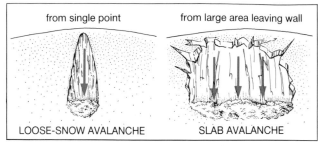

Figure 7.8 Types of avalanche

Figure 7.9a Loose snow avalanche

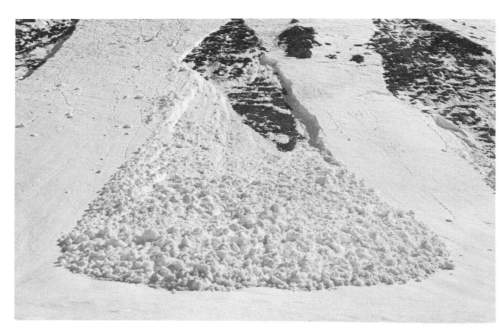

b Slab avalanche

snow breaks away leaving a backwall of ice and snow. The slab then glides downhill on a sliding surface.

Once started an avalanche can move in two ways:

1 **Flowing avalanche**: where it 'flows' over the surface.

2 **Airborne-powder avalanche**: where it moves as dry powder through the air.

ACTIVITIES

11 Figure 7.9 shows the two types of avalanche. Make a sketch of the photograph and label each type. Also label the 'backwall' and the 'sliding surface'.

Can avalanches be prevented?

On a steep slope with no vegetation snow can move freely. Methods can be used to prevent this. Trees will stabilise snow cover and will form obstructions to moving snow. Structures made of wood or metal can be built to prevent the downward movement of snow. Figure 7.10 shows some of these structures.

Further down the slope a number of structures can be built to divert avalanches away from property. Figure 7.11 shows a structure built to divert avalanches to the sides of a restaurant!

In Switzerland avalanche maps have been produced for tourist areas. These show the danger zones, where avalanches are most likely to occur. Switzerland also has a warning and evacuation system involving helicopters and specially trained army units.

Figure 7.10 Structures for preventing avalanches

Figure 7.11 Protecting a restaurant from possible avalanches

Subsidence

Figure 7.12 shows a house up-ended after the land surface has collapsed into underground salt mines; this collapse is called **subsidence**. Although few people actually get killed, land subsidence causes a great deal of damage to houses, roads, railways and pipelines.

There are many causes of subsidence. Collapse into underground mines is common in Britain as the removal of large quantities of salt and coal create space into which the rocks above can collapse. If buildings fail to have solid foundations they may lean like the famous leaning tower of Pisa. Underground liquid exerts pressure on overlying rocks so that if the liquid is extracted the rocks are liable to subside. This has happened in California where 9,000 square kilometres of land have been affected by subsidence following water extraction. The same applies to oil. Natural weathering of limestone forms underground caverns whose roofs could collapse.

In Britain the main cause of subsidence is coal mining. Figure 7.13 shows the effect on the surface of the mining of part of a coal seam. Subsidence damages property, disrupts pipelines and causes cracks in roads, as witnessed by the M1 motorway in Nottinghamshire.

The National Coal Board has had to pay compensation to people whose houses have been damaged. In some cases the houses have had to be re-built. Underground mining techniques have been changed so that wide pillars of coal are left unmined, to support the rocks above. Another strategy is packing waste into old galleries to prevent roof collapse.

Figure 7.12 The effect of subsidence on a house in Cheshire

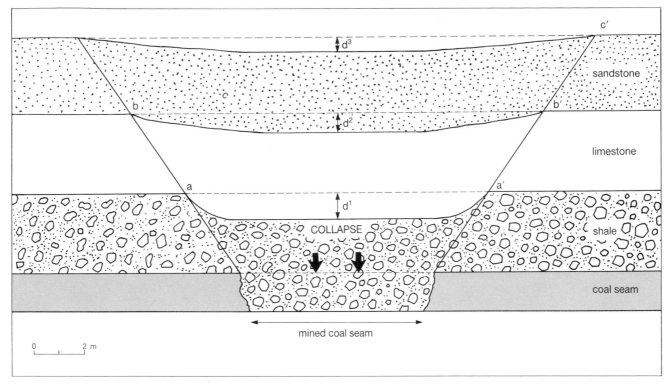

Figure 7.13 Coal mining subsidence

ACTIVITIES

12 Figure 7.14 shows compensation paid by the National Coal Board in the Barnsley area in 1977–78. Complete the table and draw a pie chart to show the information.

Repairs Compensation	Number	Percentages	Degrees
up to £250	576		
£250–£500	638		
£501–£1,000	501		
£1,001–£2,500	195		
£2,501–£5,000	51		
£5,001 and over	41		
Total		100%	360°

Figure 7.14

Note: To find percentages divide each figure by the total and multiply by 100. To find degrees, for the pie chart, multiply the percentages by 3.6.

13 a Study Figure 7.13. What is the thickness of the coal seam?

b What is the amount of collapse of the upper surface of the shale? (d_1)

c Why does your answer for b differ from your answer to a?

d Write out and complete the following table:

Layer of rock	Vertical collapse (metres)	Horizontal extent of collapse (metres)
Shale	$d_1 =$	a-a' =
Limestone	$d_2 =$	b-b' =
Sandstone	$d_3 =$	c-c' =

e Copy the paragraph below, choosing words from the list to fill in the spaces:

more   surface   less   decrease
increases   coal   seam

The table shows that the greatest vertical collapse occurs nearest the _____ and that it gradually becomes _____ moving towards the ground surface. The horizontal extent of collapse, however, actually _____ moving towards the ground surface.

f Another location has a worked out coal seam identical to that in Figure 7.13, except that it is much deeper below the ground surface. How might surface subsidence differ?

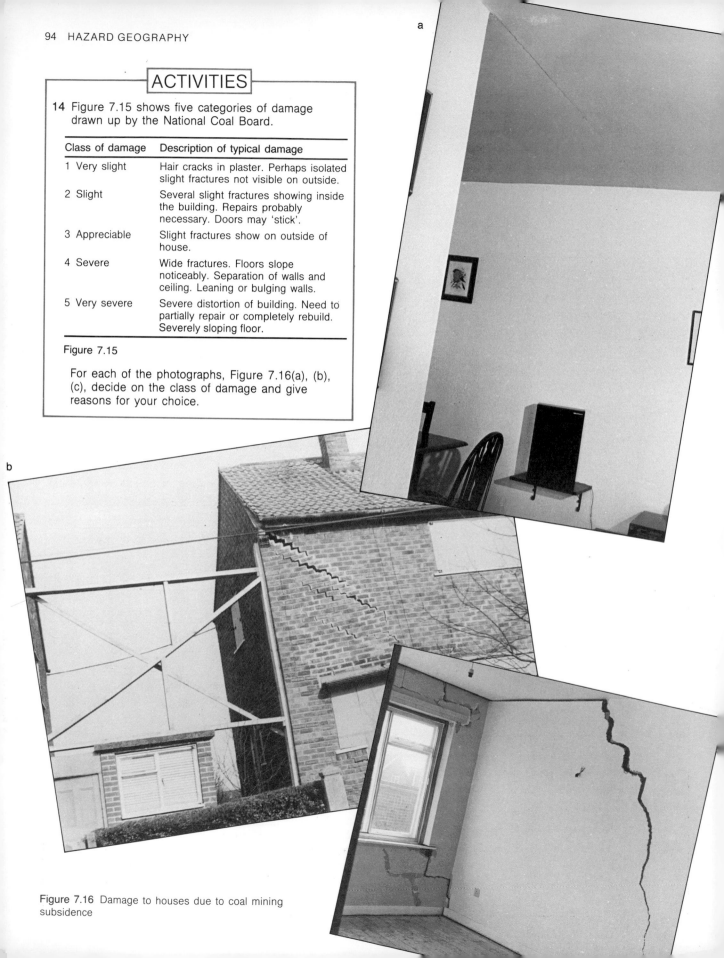

ACTIVITIES

14 Figure 7.15 shows five categories of damage drawn up by the National Coal Board.

Class of damage	Description of typical damage
1 Very slight	Hair cracks in plaster. Perhaps isolated slight fractures not visible on outside.
2 Slight	Several slight fractures showing inside the building. Repairs probably necessary. Doors may 'stick'.
3 Appreciable	Slight fractures show on outside of house.
4 Severe	Wide fractures. Floors slope noticeably. Separation of walls and ceiling. Leaning or bulging walls.
5 Very severe	Severe distortion of building. Need to partially repair or completely rebuild. Severely sloping floor.

Figure 7.15

For each of the photographs, Figure 7.16(a), (b), (c), decide on the class of damage and give reasons for your choice.

Figure 7.16 Damage to houses due to coal mining subsidence

References and further reading

Chapter 1   *Earthquakes*

Geological Museum, *Earthquakes*, HMSO, 1983.

A visit to the Geological Museum, London, is well worthwhile, especially to experience the earthquake simulation machine.

Chapter 2   *Volcanoes*

Francis, P., *Volcanoes*, Penguin, 1976; Geological Museum, *Volcanoes*, HMSO, 1974.

Chapter 3   *Flooding*

Delderfield, E.R., *The Lynmouth Flood Disaster*, RED Publications Ltd, Exeter, 1978; Smith, K. and Tobin, G.A., *Human Adjustments to the Flood Hazard*, Longman, 1979.

Regional water authorities publish details about local floods and flood protection schemes. The Flood Hazard Research Centre at Middlesex Polytechnic produces many interesting publications.

Chapter 4   *Drought*

Doornkamp, J.C. and Gregory, K.J., 'The Great Drought Recorded', *Geographical Magazine*, vol. L11, no. 4, January 1980, p. 297; Harrison, P., *Inside the Third World*, Penguin, 1979; Oxfam public affairs, *Drought and the Sahel*, Oxfam.

A great deal of interesting and up-to-date information is available from the various charity organisations. The Centre for World Development Education produces a large selection of Third World publications. For British droughts it is worth approaching the water authorities for information. The Royal Meteorological Society at Bracknell publishes detailed weather maps and an excellent magazine *Weather*.

Chapter 5   *Strong winds*

The Tornado and Storm Research Organisation, 54 Frome Road, Bradford-on-Avon monitor tornadoes in Britain. The *Journal of Meteorology* (available from the same address) is an excellent source of information.

The Royal Meteorological Society's magazine *Weather* frequently has useful articles. The National Oceanic and Atmospheric Administration (NOAA) in the USA produces material on hurricanes and tornadoes in that country.

Chapter 6   *Pollution*

Barrett, C.F. *et al.*, *Acid Deposition in the United Kingdom*, Warren Springs Laboratory, Stevenage, 1983; Fagan, J.J., *The Earth Environment*, Prentice-Hall, 1974; Holliman, J., *Waste Age Man*, Wayland Publishers Ltd, 1974; Price, B., *Friends of the Earth Guide to Pollution*, FOE, 1984.

There are a great many sources of information, the following being just a selection: Friends of the Earth; Department of the Environment; local authorities, for information on pollution control and waste disposal; water authorities, for information on water pollution; oil companies, for information on oil pollution; Central Electricity Generating Board, for details on air pollution.

Chapter 7   *Surface instability*

Fraser C., *The Avalanche Enigma*, John Murray, 1966.

The Department of Energy and the National Coal Board produce information on subsidence. Local authorities would supply information on the landslide hazard.

General bibliography

Burton, I., Katets, R.W. and White, G.F., *The Environment as Hazard*, OUP, 1978; Gribbin, J., *This Shaking Earth*, Sidgwick and Jackson, 1975; Gribbin, J., *Weather Force*, Hamlyn, 1979; Keller, E.A., *Environmental Geology*, Charles E. Merrill, 1976; Perry, A. H., *Environmental Hazards in the British Isles*, Allen and Unwin, 1981; Strahler, A.N., *Physical Geography*, John Wiley, 1975; Tank, R.W., *Focus on Environmental Geology*, OUP, 1976; Whitlow, J., *Disasters*, Penguin, 1980.

Index